WOMEN ARE CHANGING
THE CORPORATE
LANDSCAPE

Rules for cultivating
leadership excellence

WOMEN ARE CHANGING
THE CORPORATE
LANDSCAPE

Rules for cultivating
leadership excellence

BY

Jean Otte
Rosina L. Racioppi
Jill L. Ferguson

WOMEN Unlimited, Inc. · 2009

Published by
WOMEN Unlimited, Inc.
328 White Road
Little Silver, NJ 07739
(212) 572-6211
women-unlimited.com

Printed in the United States of America

First Printing: April 2009
1 3 5 7 9 10 8 6 4 2

ISBN: 978-0-9815360-0-2
Library of Congress Control Number:
2008912183

Jacket design and illustrations by Subset Design,
Ithinand Tubkam, and Edward J. Kamholz
Book interior design by Edward J. Kamholz

Acknowledgements

We so appreciate the willingness of each of the persons featured in this book who took the time to share their expertise with regard to cultivating leadership excellence. Each of you is changing the corporate landscape and your contribution will most certainly help others to continue to cultivate their leadership excellence. We thank Lesley Andrews, Sandy Beach Lin, Laura Browne, Kathleen Cashman, Catalyst, Michelle Chiantera, Donna Coulson, Michele Donato, Mark Emkes, Gina Flaig,Nicola Foster, Elaine Fotiadis, Amy Gonzales, Lesley Gustafson, Deb Hornell, Susan Kendrick, Pat Kirkland, Kim Lam, Dr. Tieraona Low Dog, Kathryn Maher, Dovie Majors, Bonnie McAreavy, Charmaine McClarie, Lee E. Miller, Velma Monteiro-Tribble, Linda Neuman, Lynley Noviello, Laure E. Park, Dev Patel, Vicki Pratt, Claudia Ruffin, Tammy Savoie, Mary Scott, Susan Sobbott, Angela Szymusiak, Patty Watson, Val Williams, Dianna D. Wilusz, and Jack Yurish. Without you and your participation WOMEN Unlimited would not be the company it is. We are also so grateful to the many organizations that partner with us and support the program participants, mentors, and managers featured in this book. Additionally, we extend a special thank you to Christopher C. Bernard for his editing skills.

Contents

Dedication

To all of the organizations that partner with WOMEN Unlimited to cultivate leadership excellence, and to the men and women in those organizations who are changing the corporate landscape.

Introduction

Twenty years ago, as I was winding down my career after over thirty years in corporate America, I had a seed of an idea—which stemmed from my own experiences and observations, mistakes and lessons learned—to create an organization to help women become successful in the corporate world. As I thought about my next steps, I reflected on the key lessons I would share and how they could be used to encourage women.

I had learned "the rules"—both written and unwritten—that every organization has and that everyone needs to understand if he or she is going to play the business game. I identified and developed my strengths and understood areas I needed to improve. I knew how to ask for and appreciate feedback. I learned that I did not need to do it alone, I didn't need to have all the answers and I should ask for help. I discovered that results are not gender-based. I learned that by working collaboratively with others and not always needing to be the "star", but a support to a winning team, we all could be winners in the business game. And finally, I realized that if a group of talented women from diverse backgrounds and experiences came together towards a common goal to be more successful leaders, willing to share their accomplishments and mistakes and to be supportive of one another, we would become a powerful force.

Fifteen years ago my vision of creating the Women's Organization for Mentoring, Education and Networking, or WOMEN Unlimited, Inc., became a reality when I was able to gain the support of seven major corporations headquartered in New York and New Jersey. I promised these corporate partners that the women they selected to participate in the unique development opportunity I had created would gain a broader business perspective and a greater understanding of how to become more successful leaders in their organizations.

But I didn't solely approach corporations. Of the eighteen women in our first New York program, three of them were scholarship participants from not-for-profit organizations. Those scholarships (which continue to be offered in our programs nationwide) were created to honor my sister Kathy, who, in her short life, devoted herself to helping women through a career in social services. I knew firsthand that the highly talented and dedicated women in not-for-profit organizations didn't have access to many of the ongoing learning opportunities available to women in corporate America, but that their perspectives would be invaluable for the corporate participants, and vice versa.

Over the years, WUI has become a nationally acclaimed leadership development organization, featured in printed publications, on television, and on radio. In 1996 when *Business Week* featured WUI and Colgate-Palmolive, one of our first Corporate Partners, the article stated that WUI was helping women in corporate America to learn "how to get the boys to pass them the ball" and other business "rules". Inquiries soon flooded our offices from people wanting to know more about how WUI went about helping women to learn those "rules".

We now partner with many of the most admired corporations in the world and have been acknowledged as a preferred provider and a key factor in assisting these organizations with leadership and diversity initiatives and talent retention. Many of our participants over the past fifteen years have become presidents and senior executives of their respective organizations, and those who "graduated" from corporate life have gone on to form their own successful companies. Most gratifying to me is how many of our graduates continue to stay connected with WUI.

Over seven thousand women have gone through our programs and achieved their objectives. When I had a vision of what would make the learning experience unique, I realized I needed a structure similar to Weight Watchers. We needed women who wanted to participate in a long-term development experience. Our Corporate Partners found these women for us by selecting the right candidates at the right time in their careers. The participants shared their goals and helped each other to reach these goals, but the ultimate success lay within each woman. Similar to a program which doesn't force people to lose weight but provides a positive, encouraging environment for people to do so, I envisioned that WUI would create the climate and provide the support, but the program would be self-directed and the women themselves would do the work needed to become more successful.

To that end, WOMEN Unlimited offers three programs developed to help women, identified as high potential by their companies, to manage the transitions of their career progression. The first program we started was the LEAD Program. Through the LEAD Program (Leadership Education and Development), women gain insight into the subtle shifts that will help them transition from tactical managers into strategic leaders. This program is for women with seven or more years of tactical management experience who are poised to move into a broader leadership role. Several years after the launch of our initial program, CPs as well as managers of participants asked for a similar program for women earlier in their career path. In response, the TEAM Program was created. The TEAM Program (Training for Emerging and Aspiring Managers) is a six-month management development program that helps women understand the competencies that will enable them to shift successfully from individual contributors to managers. The program benefits women with two or less years of managerial experience or project leadership. Around the same time the CPs were asking for what became the TEAM Program, they also requested a program for their highest-level female executives. The FEW Program (The Forums for Executive Women) is an invitation-only assembly that brings together a select group of senior women from diverse occupations and organizations to develop strategies for succeeding in the current business climate.

Each WUI program operates on the premise that the women come once a month to a safe environment where they can share their career goals, benchmark best practices and have ongoing support. We created a unique learning environment that challenges women to evaluate their leadership skills and share their strengths and challenges. They assist each other in creating plans to reach their goals. Throughout the programs we introduce various techniques and proven strategies to assist them. One important aspect of our programs is the multiple methodologies we have for holding the women accountable for what they have learned, requiring them to put these methodologies into practice to examine the results, then come back to the program each month to discuss their feedback.

We don't use traditional training methods, nor do we have a classroom atmosphere. Instead, WUI creates a facilitated learning environment that supports open discussions to determine strengths and weaknesses of certain strategies. Then, as a group, we offer suggestions/recommendations for the person to consider or try.

As the participants graduate from our programs they take great pride in sharing their achievements; a definite and increased confidence and a more positive "can do" attitude can be observed.

As you read this book you will learn the WOMEN Unlimited Inc. rules of the game for cultivating leadership excellence. These are ten simple yet effective guidelines. You may discover that you are already using these rules to your advantage. Or, you may reflect that you are "warming the bench" a little too often when you really should be in the game. Remember: You have to be in it to win it.

I encourage you all to enjoy the game.

Warm regards,

Jean

When I met Jean over fifteen years ago, I was Director of Human Resources for Degussa Corporation. Jean shared with me her vision for WOMEN Unlimited and how the program would be beneficial to the high potential women in my organization. She discussed critical business skills, such as leveraging strategic alliances, requesting feedback, and not being afraid to ask for what you want. WUI was without fancy marketing materials, but companies saw the power this type of development program would have on their organizations and the women who participated.. I immediately saw WUI's value and quickly piloted two women into the program. Jean also asked me to participate as a mentor, which provided me another perspective on the program and gave me an opportunity to further my own development.

I also benefited personally from my association with WUI, meeting mentors from diverse backgrounds and expanding my business perspective along with my network. My admiration for Jean and the organization she created increased, and our professional relationship grew into a personal friendship, which resulted in my joining WUI over twelve years ago.

During my pre-WUI career in Human Resources, part of my responsibility was managing training and development. Like many companies, we used several external resources to develop and train our staff.

Whenever someone attended one of these programs, I would follow up to determine how valuable the experience was for the individual and what impact it would have on the organization. Time and again I was disappointed when we couldn't determine a specific measurable impact to the organization or to our employees who had gone through the programs. When I would ask the employees about the experience, I typically would hear, "It was great." But when I pressed for specifics, they struggled to articulate the value.

I was also aware that many people were confused or lacked a clear direction in regards to their career paths. In some technical areas, employees were "tracked" to get promoted after a certain time in grade, which worked well until the individual reached a plateau or needed to choose between a technical track or a management track for the rest of their careers. People grew frustrated with their choices and most often abdicated the decision to their managers or someone else. During my career I witnessed many employees become frustrated with their jobs and play a waiting game, waiting for someone to "give them" their next opportunity.

A shift in this mindset was wonderful to witness, and it came with the women that we selected to participate in the initial pilot for WOMEN Unlimited. One of the most noticeable changes was that the women took back ownership of their career progression, not only owning their jobs but also being clear about what they saw as the next steps for their careers. They then actively pursued those opportunities, seeking out key individuals to discuss what they saw as the next role for them, being clear to ask for what they wanted and then asking others for feedback. Not surprisingly, they each charted courses for their careers and those courses played to their strengths, resulting in jobs they truly enjoyed and creating a win-win for both the individual and the organization.

When talking with the participants in the program about critical success strategies for women, we often get into great conversations about the issues of networking and asking for what you want. When discussing how important the skill of networking is to their business success, I often hear how these women don't have time and how their work should speak for itself. I receive similar reactions when discussing how important it is to be clear about what they want and to let it be known in their organizations. It is at this time that I enjoy sharing how Jean launched WUI, since it is a wonderful example of these critical success factors in action. Throughout Jean's career, she built a large network. When she decided to launch WUI, she reached out to this network and shared her vision. Having strategic alliances was key to her success as an executive, and was equally important as she started her own business. Equally critical to her success was being able to ask, with confidence, for people to support her company and identify women to attend the program. What started with eighteen women in the first LEAD program in 1994 has grown to thousands of women attending WUI programs; I can't think of a better story to illustrate the power of using your network and asking for what you want.

When I joined WUI in 1996, I was curious about how the women used the acumen acquired through their experiences with WOMEN Unlimited within their organizations. How did they work with their managers? Were their managers helpful to them in using the insights they had gained? What could their managers do to be more helpful to them during the program? How could we assist our Corporate Partners to become more aware of what these women learned through our programs so that they could leverage these lessons into their organizations?

I began working more closely with our Corporate Partners to advise them in their selection process to ensure that they were identifying the right woman at the right time for the right program. Over the years, our corporate partners have evolved their selection strategies, which has resulted in WUI programs becoming key for developing and retaining their high potential women.

Based on the enriching experiences I had when I was a mentor in the program, I worked very closely with our CPs to identify executive-level men and women who could be mentors in our LEAD program. And taking on this role in our program provides the opportunity for the executives to learn and develop new skills, too. When I travel to the graduations of the LEAD programs around the country, I am always interested in learning what value the mentors received through the experience. Typically I hear about the value of having a senior co-mentor from a different industry, how it is a gift to have another senior person to share ideas, etc. From the male mentors, I often hear about the insight they gained, in particular that they formulated a greater awareness of the challenges and obstacles that women face in the workplace, and how these same issues/challenges are present in their organizations.

Over the past twelve years, I have been fortunate to participate in the journey taken by the women in our programs. I see them discover their strengths and craft their paths, each month growing in knowledge and learning from their peers. All people involved in our programs—the corporate partners, the managers and the mentors—share how their development is enriched through their involvement in WUI programs.

It is my honor to share with you the Rules for Cultivating Leadership Excellence that WUI has identified as critical for your personal success, as well as your organization's success. You are invited to hear the stories of the women who have attended our programs, as well as those stories of the managers and mentors who supported them. We also have included messages from senior leaders who not only value developing a diverse talent pipeline, but see participation in WUI programs as a critical business strategy for the advancement of their organizations.

I invite you to participate in A Call to Action at the end of each chapter. Consider your career goals as you are reading each chapter and how each rule may enable you to show up more effectively in your organization. The questions presented offer you an opportunity to explore how you are cultivating your leadership excellence.

I hope these stories will inspire you just as these women and men have inspired me. Wishing you much success as you cultivate your leadership excellence.

Rosina

Rule #1:
Know the Rules

Every organization has its own rules of the business game. Rosina shares that in each of WUI's development programs, we focus the women's attention on understanding the rules of the game and how these rules can enable them to show up more effectively and more powerfully in their organizations.

When women participate in the WUI programs we give them a challenge: at graduation, tell us what you have learned and how you are applying it in your workplace to show tangible benefits of our programs. One team said their primary lesson was that they now knew the rules of being effective leaders, what they called the unspoken rules. With all of the trainings they had gone to before, no one had told them the unspoken rules of business, things like speaking with conviction and clarity, becoming a crucial associate, making decisions, taking risks, supporting the corporate value system. These are the things no one ever talks about; they are not in employee manuals. But these rules are how things

> You *have to learn the* *rules of the game, and* *then you have to play* *better than anyone else.*
>
> Albert Einstein

are done; they impact how you present yourself in an organization, and they are essential to the game of business.

In a 2008 study called " Unwritten Rules: What You Don't Know Can Hurt Your Career", written by Laura Sabattini for Catalyst, a nonprofit membership organization working globally with businesses and the professions to build inclusive workplaces and expand opportunities for women and business, says that the rules are behaviors that "take for granted as what successful employees do." (For more information on Catalyst or to read the study in its entirety, visit www.catalyst.org.)

Though what successful employees do changes slightly from company to company, some things remain constant. Successful employees are great communicators, they take advantage of developmental opportunities, they network, and they are fully engaged. A *Business Week* article in 2002, "She's Gotta Have 'It" explores why more women aren't in the leadership pipeline. Writer Michelle Conlin discusses the growing mound of research that shows that female execs trounce men in nearly every area of performance. But many lack executive presence. Cynthia Scott, a partner in San Francisco-based executive coaching firm, Changeworks, says she is "astounded at how often females in danger of being written off for advancement will leave a meeting without having said much. That makes them come off as passive and unengaged."

Jean says she asks WUI participants if she gave them a new board game with no rules included, what would they do? Most participants say they would make up the rules. Jean says, she believes this is true of many women in the business world, who rather than admit they don't know what the rules of the game are, they would rather go it alone and try to play the game without knowing the rules. Jean shares that in her early days in the business world this is what she often did until she realized it wasn't working out for her and that it made much more sense to find out from others what the game was really about. Jean says, "Asking for help is difficult for many women. But many women who are new to business don't realize it is a real game being played in their organizations, with already established rules." Some of these rules are explicitly stated in employee handbooks or by senior leadership, but many of the rules are implicit, or unwritten.

SUIT UP PROPERLY

Another component of understanding the rules involves knowing what you are bringing to the table, and if you are suited up properly. You wouldn't bring a lacrosse stick to play field hockey nor would you wear football pads while figure skating. Each employee needs a business arsenal, comprised of the skills and talents she brings to her organization. Each employee also needs mentors who can provide guidance and counsel that helps to broaden business perspectives. The arsenal will grow over the course of your career and the rules will slightly change. When you become a leader in your organization, you will need a broader picture and a broader approach. This is a part of those unspoken rules. Rosina remembers talking with a company president regarding one of his senior level employees. The president expressed concern about the manner this executive was discussing his view of recent changes to the company benefit plan. The executive's behavior, how he chose to share his opinion, was not reflective of a senior level executive. The president shared how his view of this person had changed and this impacted what future opportunities would be offered. The behavior that worked for you as a new employee may not work for you as you navigate your career. Do you know what kind of unwritten behavioral rules are enforced by your company? When you face resistance to your ideas is it because you are going against one of the rules?

In her books, author Gail Evans refers to rules by which every organization plays the game of business, but she points out that most of these rules were written by men. Rosina says, "In 2009, women should be better at this gamesmanship, but it continues to be a challenge for us." We need to know the rules, work within the rules, and not judge them, as wasting time judging them will hinder our effectiveness.

LET YOUR INSTINCTS GUIDE YOU

Susan Sobbott, President of American Express OPEN, says that in figuring out part of the unwritten rules, you should let your instincts guide you. "Every day we navigate complex social situations in our lives that are governed by sophisticated rules. We've not learned them formally in a classroom or from a book. We've simply followed our instincts, using observation and experience to guide us. Similarly, every company has its own culture, with its own etiquette of unwritten rules. Learning these rules requires that you listen to your instincts and have the confidence to trust your own observations and insights. Some of the rules will be immediately apparent, but others may only be clear in hindsight. In fact, you'll likely learn a few rules by accidentally breaking them. But if you become a student of your environment—and have the resilience to bounce back when you've made a false step along the way— you'll have learned an essential skill that defines success. Because wherever your career takes you, there will always be new and evolving rules to learn."

Jean says she realized business is a game when she

observed how her male colleagues and bosses approached their work. "They told me I was taking things too personally, rather than just accepting the fact that sometimes you win, sometimes you tie, and sometimes you lose." And each of these—winning, tying, and losing—are essential learning experiences.

UNDERSTAND THE DECISION-MAKING PROCESS IN YOUR ORGANIZATION

Sobbott says, "The most important unwritten rules in any company relate to decision-making. Without an understanding of these rules, even the most carefully made plans and detailed preparation are meaningless."

Sobbott provides this example: "Several years ago, a young employee came to the company as a top graduate from a prestigious MBA program. She immediately set high goals for an ambitious new project, did extensive research, and diligently drew up detailed strategies to support her plan. She built a strong argument to win the budget she needed, and entered the meeting confident and armed with facts, figures, and well-crafted rebuttals. But she was faced with the unexpected. When the topic of her proposal came to the table, decision-makers showed little interest in her project. Despite her attempts to sway opinion, a consensus quickly arose and funding was awarded to other priorities. Without proper financial backing, her plans were hopelessly derailed."

"When she asked my advice," Sobbott remarks, "I asked her to describe what she thought had gone wrong. For her, the most troubling idea was that she felt people's minds were made up before hearing her argument. What went wrong? Her decision-makers met with the unexpected. The first they heard of her great idea was when she asked for the 'yes.' She suddenly understood one of the rules of decision-making. Her extensive preparation was well founded, but her timing was off. She needed to present her case one-on-one with decision-makers to build familiarity and consensus before the meeting."

Charmaine McClarie, President of the McClarie Group, refers to what she calls Trap #1: Being Politically Blindsided by an Organization You Don't Understand. McClarie says to look around your workplace and pay attention. "Who gets seen and heard in your organization? Who is highly respected?" she asks, and why do people listen to them?. "Who is a great contributor but goes unnoticed? Who has great insight but is ignored? Why don't people listen to them?"

We've all had this happen or have seen it happen, when the best-prepared plans seem to be sidetracked or even plowed over by others in our organizations. We need to stop and think about why this occurs. Jean recalls that one boss told her, "Despite your best efforts you are going to miss the throw or fumble the ball. It doesn't mean you are not capable; it's just the way the game can go on a given day."

Think about these things in order to be better prepared for the next pass. Sobbott advises, "Look at how decisions are made in your company. Are they made one person at a time or by committee? Who makes the decision, and who influences the outcome? What criteria are used? In what manner should a proposal be presented? When is a good time to ask for a decision, and when are the times to avoid? And when is the decision really made? As you observe, you will begin to see patterns that explain the rules of decision-making in your company. Also, supplement your personal observations by learning from others. Colleagues are an important source for you. When your goals rely on the outcome of a particular decision, don't hesitate to ask the opinion of those you trust. They can often shed light on the rules by suggesting ways to influence decisions. And some may also be willing to share insightful stories about their own experiences."

80% of success is showing up.

Woody Allen

CREDIBILITY IS THE KEY

"From the playground to the boardroom, all groups

have tacit rules that determine which individuals are heard. Credibility is key to influencing others. A few years ago, a colleague of mine came to the company with the reputation of a rising star." Sobbott recalls, "He was known for a high-profile success and hoped to quickly produce results in his new position. The first big move he made was to propose a highly profitable expansion of an existing product. He had done all the research, evaluating the market opportunity and the details of competitive products. But when he presented his case to upper management—many of whom he was meeting for the first time—they simply weren't convinced. It was a crushing defeat.

"In his previous company, leaning on a robust track record and using a streamlined approach worked well, so he made his presentation using headlines and glossed over much of the supporting data. But at his present company his shorthand wasn't trusted because he hadn't earned the right to use it. A new leader presenting a new idea needs to prove his or her comprehensive thinking and to show that the detailed homework was done. Credibility itself is built by knowing the rules. In this case, understanding the decision-making criteria builds credibility. The colleague in this example hadn't learned that numbers would speak loudest to his audience in this decision, especially when he, the recommender of a new idea, was an unknown quantity to the decision-makers. To help him build credibility, I suggested that he present his case again with much more financial detail, and I also advised him to ask a supportive senior colleague to join him. His second attempt was a success."

Sobbott adds, "Credibility is often earned by following unspoken rules, such as backing statements and claims with the right kind of information, whether it's data or the support of others. Study the people in your company who command the most respect and compare what they have in common. What's their professional background, how healthy are their relationships with others, and who are their most apparent allies? People's credibility often relies on accomplishments, such as the importance of their responsibilities, their latest successes, or simply seniority. In some organizations, outside recognition speaks loudly: who has been published the most, and who has received the most recognition in the press? Seemingly simple work habits can also command attention and respect. For example, are the most credible people in your company good listeners? Are they open to discussion and debate? And do they favor a collaborative approach? Credibility flows from many sources, and it's up to you to uncover the rules that will bring you respect and influence in your company."

BE ARTICULATE AND
STAND UP FOR YOURSELF

Mark Emkes, CEO of Bridgestone Americas, a WUI Corporate Partner who has sent more than one hundred women through our programs, offers these guidelines for the game of business: "My advice to any woman who aspires to a leadership position in an organization is very similar to what I would advise anyone—male or female—who seeks to succeed: always respect people; show people that you care (and mean it!); work hard to eliminate confusion; keep people informed; and always keep learning. I've found one of the best ways to keep learning is to read, read, and then read some more, especially biographies and books on leadership.

"But there is one tendency that I've observed in a number of women executives that I think bears mentioning. For whatever reason, I've seen women with great ideas articulate them, but then once challenged by others (especially men), defer to them, even if the women know in their hearts that their ideas are the better ones. You need to trust in yourself and in your judgment, and speak up! By politely but firmly standing up for your ideas and yourself, you're benefiting the organization of which you're a part, and you're developing the leadership skills you'll need to succeed for the long term. In my experience, the women executives I've known are very logical and possess great common sense. Sometimes they just need to be a bit more forceful about letting their audiences know about their good sense and great ideas."

TAKE CHARGE OF YOUR DEVELOPMENT, AND FOLLOW THE RULES

Sandra Beach Lin, Executive Vice President at Celanese Corporation and President of Ticona (a business of Celanese), says that the rules for being a senior executive in the corporate landscape include knowing how to leverage the capabilities and skills that got you to that level, and knowing that those will not be enough. "Continuous learning and development are vital to success at the top echelon. You are responsible for your own development and at this level, you should clearly be focused on talent development for your company," she says.

Another part of the rules is understanding the corporate culture and then understanding how to be successful in that culture. "The stakes are higher at senior levels, the risks are higher, and the rewards are higher, so know how to work the culture to enhance your success and that of your company," Beach Lin points out. "And take the time to learn about compensation at senior levels to ensure that you negotiate successfully for yourself." Two other key strategies Beach Lin sees as vital to understanding the rules of business at the executive level are to acknowledge the importance of peer relationships, and to speak up. "Weigh in, influence, and be persuasive," she says. By adopting these rules—both written and unwritten—women are changing the corporate landscape.

SUMMARY:

Successful Leaders...

1. Choose the game best suited for their skills and passion.

2. Determine the written and unwritten rules of the game in their organization to become a successful player.

3. Determine how their role/skills support the organization's mission.

4. Are students of the organizational environment to more fully understand the value system in their organizations.

5. Observe those who are MVP's, what they do that is valued, how they are valued and rewarded.

6. Commit to continuous learning and take responsibility for their continued growth and development.

WOMEN ARE CHANGING THE CORPORATE LANDSCAPE

CALL TO ACTION:

● Identify one strategy that demonstrates your understanding of the rules of the game in your organization.

● Identify two key individuals who effectively demonstrate an in-depth understanding of your organization's rules of the game and set up a meeting with them to gain greater insight.

● Determine what resources (industry publications, etc.) are available and can be used to strengthen your understanding of your business or industry.

● Meet with a colleague who has a very different role than you in the organization so you can gain a broader business perspective.

OTTE · RACIOPPI · FERGUSON

NOTES

Rule #2:
Assess Your Impact

In this game we play called business, it is important that each of us is very aware of the skills we bring to this game and how they help us to play and win. It is also important to recognize the need to constantly assess and upgrade our skill set as we play more challenging and complex games. The skills we used as children to skip rope are not those we need to play double-dutch.

Rosina shares, "This makes me think of my daughter Danielle who played field hockey in middle school and as a freshman in high school. The first two years she played, she was afraid of the ball, and this fear caused her not to be as confident as she needed to be. This year she is on the junior varsity team at her high school. The try-outs were more competitive and she was thrilled to make the team. Danielle knew that she needed to get over her fear of the ball if she was going to play well and keep her spot on the team.

> *Not only is it the most difficult thing to do, but sometimes the most inconvenient.*
> John Gardner

"When I went to her first game, I saw a new person on the field. She was more assertive and played more strategically. Afterwards, I asked her what was different this year. She said, 'I realized that I just had to get over my fears or I would not grow and be the kind of player that is valued on the team. After all, I am playing at a different level.'"

One of the biggest challenges people have at work is taking a step back and really seeing themselves through the eyes of others. How do other people see you? Are you an available player? How are you impacting your organization? Do you impact the correct areas of the company, the areas the organization's leaders currently are emphasizing?

As Jean thinks about the business game, she is convinced that every day the game begins anew. With that in mind, it is so important to take the time to assess how you impacted the game yesterday and how you plan to play the game today. It also is imperative that in addition to asking yourself how you believe you did, that you ask others how they think you did. Look at what you are doing and how it supports the mission of your organization. How often do you ask your peers, co-workers, managers, etc. how you are doing? What can you do better? How can you better help them? Continually seeking answers to these questions will help keep you on track and avoid the derailments that can happen when people work in a vacuum—just doing what they feel is important and doing it in the way they feel is best. How often people are surprised at performance review time or when they participate in a 360-degree assessment to find their view of their performance does not match that of their boss.

ASSESS YOUR TALENTS AND SKILLS AND LEVERAGE THEM

We need to ask which of our talents are unique. What sets us apart from others? These talents often drive our initiatives towards success. Can we articulate those talents or skill sets and promote them?

Women aren't always mindful of the talents that enable our success. We just do things—many things—without thinking much about what we are doing and how it impacts our companies. Women multi-task because they are expected to and because they are used to working on so many different levels simultaneously. But we need to stop and think about what makes us successful and why our talents and skills are important parts of our organizations. We also need to think about what we enjoy doing. So often we get put into roles and we do tasks at which we excel, but we do not enjoy those tasks. Maybe we enjoyed them at one time or we did the task because we had to, but now we no longer enjoy the work and wish we could do something else. We need to be able to analyze our skills so that we can apply them towards moving in a different direction.

Then we should share those thoughts with others so that they can help us leverage our skills and talents. Assessing your impact cannot be an introspective exercise. You need to involve others. Your managers and colleagues cannot tap into you as a resource unless they know what talents you have. Oftentimes women think that letting people know what they are good at will be seen as bragging. But we need to reframe our thoughts and realize that if people don't know about us and about our skills, then how can they invite us to be vital parts of teams or projects?

By sharing with our co-workers, we receive validation and/or direction. We may think we are doing something vitally important to the company. But when we share with our managers we may find out that what we are doing doesn't have the impact we thought, or maybe we aren't affecting the part of the company that we should be. Only by assessing and then sharing with others do we receive this kind of feedback.

At the end of each day we need to ask, "What do I personally want to accomplish in my career? What do I want to—and what should I—impact in my company to help me reach that career objective? And how can I tie these two things together?"

Claudia Ruffin, WUI Program Manager for New York, describes assessing your impact in this way:

Women often come to their roles with a lot of skills to do many things. But at the end of the day, they accomplish a lot of stuff that has little to no impact. Using skills in this manner narrows their focus and keeps them in the tactical versus strategic mode (more on this in Chapter 8). To have impact, you must know the strengths/skills you bring to your role; what skills are essential for the role; and where to spend your time. Being clear about this supports how you position yourself in the game. Ask yourself what your strengths are and if the organization knows and values them. Then, assess your impact to determine if you are leveraging these strengths with behaviors that consistently demonstrate your intentions.

SOLICIT FEEDBACK

To determine how effective you are, you need the gift of feedback from others. The 360-degree feedback is one of the most useful assessment tools for gaining insight about your effectiveness and how you are perceived by others. This assessment can take place on-line or via interviews. Providing the opportunity for others (manager, direct reports, peers/colleagues, customers and others) to give you feedback—regardless of the relationship being good, bad, or indifferent—can be powerful, Ruffin says.

The power comes in what you do and how you use the results. When you are authentic with yourself and really listen to the messages in your results, you may find that it's not all new information but rather confirmation that it is time to make some subtle adjustments in how you do more or less to demonstrate your impact. In order to identify what to focus on and how to make your adjustment, you need to start by getting out of your own way. This includes ridding yourself of judgment and justification so that your mind is clear and able to flow into a neutral and creative space.

Ruffin says, to help you narrow your focus, think about the game and yourself as a player on the team. Each member of the team is given one team bag, which is the only bag to be used during the season. Considering your feedback, what would you pack in your team/organization bag? Take some time to step back and reflect on how much baggage you currently have and how long you've been carrying it around. Most people have been carrying baggage that's not theirs, not usable nor necessary for their roles. The key is to travel light and pack those essential strengths/skills that can be used in more than one way and allow you to be adaptable, flexible, and to add value. It is important to also include one skill that is crucial for your development. When you play to your strengths, other areas will be enhanced along the way. As for that additional baggage that you've been holding on to, Ruffin says to "Let it Go! It's a new season, lighten the load, and get yourself in position."

Having courage and determination to assess your impact throughout your journey is what keeps you on top of cultivating your leadership excellence and provides the foundation for you and others to change the corporate landscape.

PLAN FOR PERSONAL AND PROFESSIONAL SUCCESS

WOMEN Unlimited alum Dovie Majors, IQS Process/Integration Manager at Bridgestone Firestone North American Tire, LLC, explains how she has learned to assess her impact, how she's changed the corporate landscape, and what a difference it has made in her career, which has ranged from being a line-level employee working on equipment fourteen years ago at Bridgestone to her current management role.

"WOMEN Unlimited challenged me to understand what impact looked like in my organization. A key activity I engaged in while going through the WUI LEAD program was to dedicate one hour in my schedule each day to plan for both personal and professional success. During the course of a year, I took time to review my organization's mission, vision, and values statements and to make mental maps of what strategies were being developed to meet our CEO's vision and bottom-line business needs. I focused on understanding how policies cascaded throughout the organization to achieve the big picture. Through putting myself at this 30,000-foot view, as explained during the WUI Big League Business Thinking workshop, I began to make better sense of what value looked like in my organization. Linking the teachings of WUI, I was able to uncover some simplistic yet powerful methods for increasing my value, visibility, and vision as a leader.

"One of the key things I began focusing on in my career was to volunteer for projects or roles where a turn-around was needed, where those before me had failed, or where the role or project itself was new and needed vision. WUI taught me that projects and roles with these characteristics are highly visible in an organization. But these roles also contain risk. I have learned to see these as great opportunities to stretch and to showcase value and to demonstrate that I can develop a vision, influence others to share that vision with me, and to take on the challenge with my team, leading all of us towards success. But success must be understood this way: it is gained when my level of influence grows to the point where those I was assigned to lead have embraced the vision; where I am listening to them tell me how we achieve the vision; and where I am then focusing on removing barriers for them and following them to victory."

Majors provides this example: "I took on a project where there were leadership challenges for prior leaders. Prior barriers put the job on the radar for senior leadership. Although there was an additional focus, I felt confident that if I worked with the people in, around, and above me and motivated them to pull together and work as a team, we could succeed. I know that people want and need to be led and that people need to feel their leaders are genuine. I have found that my actions and spirit are reflected by those I lead. By starting with myself and challenging my own thoughts, motivation, and knowledge, I create an environment conducive to motivation, empowerment, and the tenacity required to overcome tough obstacles.

"From these first basic steps of commitment and dedication to understanding the business and then to becoming introspective and to managing my message (another WUI teaching), I began the journey of personal growth and development. I encouraged my team members to also go on this journey (both with me and on their own). And in six months time, our facility was the best in North America, and I made sure my team understood their impact," Majors says.

"Assessing your impact and other teachings of Jean Otte and her team are not happenstance; rather, they are well proven, yet tailored to specifically address the dynamics of women leaders. In addition to my career, I am a doctoral candidate who has begun intensive research into the study of leadership practice and scholarship. Research, from R.E. Hofman, Jr., and others, shows that conscious-authentic leadership is a unique approach of the individual leader to infuse his or her personal values, beliefs, and relational skills into leading and encouraging action. Further, according to Hofman, 'conscious-authentic leaders have the ability to choose how to enhance their own sense of reality and knowledge of self by actually challenging [and managing] the external forces that bombard them daily'.

"As a conscious-authentic leader, I challenge myself to see the realities of my leadership style and business needs. Since participating in WOMEN Unlimited, when my team has faced unthinkable challenges, I have always said, 'It is what it is.' I work to understand quickly the challenge as it is so that I can then begin the value-added work of strategically and systematically navigating a new course for success. Leadership expert John C. Maxwell reminds us that competitive advantage lies with the team that is able to see obstacles the quickest and then maneuver around them. You have to be able to embrace the ugly to begin the beautification process," Major states.

UNDERSTAND HOW YOU LAND ON OTHERS

"WUI helped me understand the power of being introspective and understanding 'how I landed on others' as Deb Hornell, Midwest WUI Regional Director, calls it. As you try to understand why it is so important to be introspective and to focus on developing yourself before being fully capable of leading or helping others, take a minute to think about the safety instructions given to you when you are on a commercial airline. Clearly and consistently, no matter which airline you are flying, the flight attendants direct you to secure the oxygen mask for yourself first before trying to assist others. Now think about that. What they are saying is true for leadership, too. You cannot effectively assist others unless you assist or develop yourself first. You assess yourself through feedback from others, then you work to manage your behavior and to manage expectations. You begin to see yourself from the perspective of your leader, your peers, your direct reports, your customers, your family—you see yourself in a 360-degree view. From there, you begin demonstrating leadership of self, which ultimately prepares you for leading others," Majors concludes.

Bruce Sevy, Director of Leadership Assessment Products at Personnel Decisions International, also talks of 360-degree assessment, explaining that it "starts with a list of the specific characteristics of high performers. This list is the basis of a performance survey that is distributed to people who have observed the individual in a variety of work settings. These individuals—typically the boss, peers, direct reports, and, perhaps, customers—are asked to rate the extent to which the employee has demonstrated the performance-related characteristics and to comment on the things the person can do (more, less, differently) to increase his/her performance. When aggregated, these performance ratings give the individual clear insight into the specific behaviors that contribute to or detract from performance. By using this feedback to identify areas of change, the individual can work to modify his/her behaviors, and through that effort, increase his/her performance."

Major agrees and says, "Through developing my communication skills (verbal, written, and non-verbal cues) I was able to begin the task of managing my message and developing long-lasting, positive relationships. Building trust is critical to being able to lead others or assist others effectively. As a leader, I have gained trust by being consistent, displaying ethical and moral behavior, building positive working relationships, and always looking inwardly and listening to common themes from the perspective of others. These are the cornerstones of what I believe my CEO, Mark Emkes, is referring to when he challenges each individual in our organization to engage in open, honest, and transparent communications to break down silos and build upon.

"Through research, experience, training, and development, I have learned that one must be introspective, humanistic, a big picture thinker, willing to do the hard jobs that have high visibility and reasonable risk, and influential through relationships rather than job title alone to be an effective leader. These are the cornerstones of leadership value. As a woman, you have to understand why the perceptions of your actions can differ drastically from those of men. It is the fine, un-written rules and dynamics between the sexes where WUI has helped me find my competitive advantage. Now, it is time for you to assess your impact and to find your competitive advantage!"

There are no mistakes, no coincidences. All events are blessings given to us to learn from.
Elisabeth Kubler-Ross

Effective leaders know the importance of soliciting feedback on a regular basis. Rosina remarks, "I am not referring to formal 360 assessment but rather the informal feedback following a meeting or project completion. Often a great challenge for women, asking for feedback in person is something we tend to avoid." We are cautious because what if we are told something we don't want to hear? But it is vital that we understand how our actions are valued and perceived by others, and after a meeting or project ends, that is the perfect opportunity to gain valuable insight. In our programs, we encourage women to identify someone whose feedback would be helpful to them. Then we ask them to approach that person and to ask for specific feedback. In order to receive valuable input, it is essential to ask a pointed question, such as: "Mary, I'm very interested in your thoughts about the meeting. What did you feel I did that worked well in the meeting?" After Mary has given feedback, then you need to ask, "What could I have done differently?" The insight gained from these informal feedback sessions is highly impactful.

SUMMARY:

Successful Leaders...

1. Continuously assess their skill set, commitment and passion.

2. Assess their contribution on a daily basis with regard to supporting their organization's game plan and mission.

3. Seek out feedback to determine their strengths and opportunity for improvement.

4. Ask for feedback to gain insight on how they are perceived by others.

CALL TO ACTION:

●Identify your key differentiators (skills/experience/leadership traits) and how these skills enable you to have a positive impact on your organization.

●Create a development plan for your ongoing growth and development. Be certain your plan includes:

●Leveraging your key differentiators—challenging yourself to take this skill to the next/higher level.

●Clear description of what success will look like when you have reached your development goal.

●Meet with two individuals who can provide you with feedback on the key areas of your development plan.

NOTES

NOTES

NOTES

Rule #3:
Don't Do It Alone

WOMEN Unlimited has observed how many women are still attempting to "go it alone". Many women who, rather than ask for guidance or tell others they are having problems, work twice as hard trying to work things out themselves. Why? Because many of these women have a belief that asking for help makes them look less competent. In reality, truly savvy employees understand asking others, who may have had similar experiences or who may have a perspective about the issues, is invaluable. Getting input from others is key to continuous growth as a leader.

> Nobody, but nobody can make it out there alone.
>
> Maya Angelou

It is a gift to have a network of people who are willing to share their experiences and to give feedback on your thoughts and recommendations. No one is ever so "all knowing" that he or she cannot learn from another's perspective. Even Tiger Woods has a coach, and he asks for input on how he can be better.

One of the first business lessons Rosina learned in

her life came from her father, John Piccotti. The morning she was leaving for her first job he said to her, "You don't get respect from just showing up. You need to earn people's respect by the way you treat them. And you need to treat everyone from the janitors to the executives with the same amount of respect." Rosina has never forgotten those words. She says, "People can let you into secret business rules, for example people's likes and dislikes and when someone has an extra few minutes to meet with you. Don't damage your image as an effective leader because of the way you treat people."

Jean adds to these sentiments in her sessions when she reminds women that everyone is equal in a company from the people in the mailroom to the administrative assistants to the managers; the only thing differentiating between people are their titles, which can be fluid. She uses the example of a par-ticular administrative assistant with whom she developed a relationship. This woman was the gatekeeper to the company CEO's time. Because of the relationship Jean cultivated with her, Jean had access to face-time with the CEO. Sometimes it was for only a few minutes—such as a call saying he's getting on the elevator now if you want to catch him—and other times more formal meetings were scheduled. But the relationship Jean had with the assistant helped foster a relationship with the company CEO, which in turn helped Jean's career bloom.

Another important aspect of not doing it alone is to remember another of Jean's favorite sayings, "It's not who you know; it's who knows you know." Talking with others about what you are working on and getting their perspectives also allows for you to be able to demonstrate your abilities. Oftentimes when you are working in your own silo, others do not have the opportunity to understand your strategy or plans to accomplish your goals. Taking the time to share your plans with others can serve as a highly beneficial tactic, not only to gain fresh viewpoints and ideas, but also to become a more visible, competent player.

ALIGN YOURSELF WITH THE RIGHT PEOPLE

Rosina advises that our careers can flourish when we align ourselves with the right people. Let's face it, no matter what level of the company we are in, sometimes it is difficult to admit when we don't know or understand something. We think that to excel we must know everything and that we need to be repositories of all knowledge. We see many women in our programs fall victim to this thinking. But by tapping into other people's expertise we will enjoy our work more since we'll have more resources and get more effective results. Women often pull inside themselves and shoulder things alone, which is unhealthy and unproductive. Instead, they should seek out mentors from all ranks of employment within the company and within the industry. Through mentoring relationships, one thing women learn is how to ask for help. Mentoring relationships also teach women how to look at things from many different angles and from various levels. This enables the mentored to see unique business solutions.

As part of our process of learning from others, in our workshops at WOMEN Unlimited we get people together from very distinct and divergent industries and have them work together on problems and mini-case studies. Doing this gives people new, broader perspectives and provides better solutions to the challenges faced in business. Each participant in WOMEN Unlimited programs is expected to put together a personal "Board of Directors", five or six people in her company and/or industry who help her look at things in a new or different way. This Board of Directors possesses a broad array of knowledge and they help take the weight of having to know everything from the participant's shoulders. This enables the woman to step back from the details of getting things done and enables them to see the bigger business issues, and the effects that their tasks and solutions have on the entire organization.

Having mentors who are on the same level as you and on different functional levels than you can challenge you and your assumptions and expand your thinking. This forces you to think about the next step in your career. Mentors also provide honest feedback on what you've done well and can challenge you to shift your behavior in a direction that will better serve your career goals. Your strategy can evolve and can have greater impact, in both your career and in your company, when you solicit others' insight.

Lynley Noviello, Operations Director for NY Global for Cisco, says, "My approach to business and to life is to be sure to see things from different perspectives so I can understand the big picture and the impact of decisions on both the short and long term, but without over-analyzing those decisions." Noviello adds that this plays into "Don't Do It Alone" because running ideas by a mentor who asks probing questions makes her look at things differently. "This is key to my decision making and from a strategic standpoint."

Lesley Gustafson, Project Manager at John Deere, has used the idea of "Don't Do It Alone" that she learned at WUI, not only in her career but also in her family and extra curricular activities. She and her brother have created the Eagle Excellence Program, which is in its third year. Eagle Excellence was developed to educate and assist students about higher education in their hometown, a small farming community in southwest Iowa. "We meet with classes to discuss our opportunities," she says, "because of our decisions to go to college and earn our bachelor's degrees. We discuss earning potential, non-monetary benefits, preparation for college, costs, financial resources, internships, and extra curricular activities. We have also funded a scholarship to assist students with achieving their four-year degrees." They also tell students how in order to go through school you really can't do it alone. And as examples, they are recruiting others to talk with classes and to contribute financially towards the scholarships. Gustafson says, "We know that with the contributions of others, this program will become something much greater than it is today.

"The concept of 'Don't Do it Alone' is basic, but not necessarily easy." It can force you outside of your comfort zone. But when we go outside our comfort zones and see things from different perspectives, we can deliver better results.

Other challenges can include when a group of people are assigned to you (as opposed to hand-picked by you), knowing the ideal timing to bring others into a project, and bringing in cross functional team members. Gustafson says that on a former assignment the team she worked with was chosen and assigned to her. "There were not enough decision makers who were able to get things done on this team." Through this experience she realized the value of being able to create her own teams. "It is important your team members understand strategic direction. And the right players need to be on the team so the team will continue the work even if you, as team leader, move onto another project," she says.

EXAMINE HOW YOU SEE AND INTERACT WITH OTHERS

Jack Yurish, President of J.L. Yurish & Assoc., WUI Board Member, and the mentor of Jean Otte, says that in order to be an effective leader, it is important for you "to examine and fully understand your own attitude about the fundamental worth and value of people. Are they assets that can appreciate and increase in value if properly led, encouraged, and invested in? Do you see the value, for the organization, as well as for your own career success, in developing crucial associates?"

Part of those unwritten rules to advancement, as defined in the Catalyst study, "Unwritten Rules: What You Don't Know Can Hurt Your Career", includes being a team player who works well with others.

Elaine Fotiadis, Director, Finance Talent

Management at Prudential, says, "Certain projects in the past I've worked on by myself and at a certain time the project needs to go out into the organization. If you wait too long to bring people in your success levels go down because they (end users, stakeholders, etc.) are less committed and the project might be perceived as 'Elaine's thing'. We need to realize that everything we do in our roles within our companies we do through others. So it is important to have effective, high performing teams."

Fotiadis says, "Part of my job is to think strategically about training and development for the organization, but I have to get buy-in from others who can implement these programs and projects. This means I need cross functional teams and senior leadership support so that our ideas and goals are aligned with what the organization wants to accomplish." Working with people from other departments and at various levels in the organization gives you a broader perspective of what is happening in all levels of the company. This can let you into insights and upcoming changes or focus-shifts that may not be widely publicized for a while, but this will help you to better align yourself with your company's values and direction.

ESTABLISH AN EXECUTIVE NETWORK

Noviello says WOMEN Unlimited's LEAD

Program helped her career by giving her an opportunity to get in front of the executives at her company, through conducting executive interviews, an exercise that is required in the WUI LEAD Program. This helped her create an executive network. "I spent the whole day with our CEO, John Chambers, hosting him on customer calls. I thought we would only be together for a brief time period but after the first meeting, John asked where we were going next and if we were going to lunch. This gave me a chance to ask him questions about leadership. He asked me during lunch what three things the company could do differently and I ruffled a few feathers when I told him what I thought. But the next time I was in town he approached me." Noviello says that because of this relationship her CEO recommended who her next mentor should be, as hers left Cisco.

But Noviello cautions anyone trying to establish an executive network not to grandstand. "Your work needs to be recognized by key stakeholders. Understand what drives and motivates others and understand how you can make an impact. And develop a support system across the whole network."

Gustafson asked her network to help before her interview with her company's CEO, Bob Lane. "Prior to our interview, my colleagues helped me to formulate a discussion regarding the opportunity for an international assignment. During the interview I was able to clearly articulate my situation and what I wanted. Applying Rule #3: Don't Do It Alone helped to progress my goal of an international assignment in Germany into reality." (Gustafson, during the summer of 2008, completed her assignment of Supply Base Manager in Mannheim, Germany, and she has returned to the States to a lead a new project.)

But never think of your network as a static entity. Your network should evolve and grow as you do. Fotiadis offers this advice: "Whenever you are brought into a new assignment or project, reassess who you need to be in a relationship with—in a one-on-one—and it will help you work together as a team if you understand each other as individuals, as opposed to just being team members."

In Gustafson's new role, she is re-examining her network, as she will be leading a team consisting of internal and external members. "Internally, it will include leading John Deere team members located in the USA, Germany, and Spain. Externally, it could lead to discussions and proposals for an acquisition or joint venture. This assignment will be an interesting challenge, and one that I will need to utilize the insight from experienced and successful colleagues in order to succeed."

Noviello says that at Cisco they do Pulse Surveys, which determine if their activities are aligned with the company's goals, objectives, and strategies. Then they use those to assign people to special task teams across the U.S. "I just helped one candidate expand outside of New York and connect with people in Colorado so that she expands her network. I help my teams figure out who their mentors should be, what their career goals are, and then to become mentors themselves. For example, Account Managers should mentor Sales Associates who are fresh out of college."

Fotiadis also has mentors and encourages others to do so, too. "Although Prudential has a formal mentoring program, I've never taken part in it because I've always had informal mentoring relationships. The department I used to work in had personal coaching circles, and that is what I informally use today, except I don't pull them together as a group." Fotiadis has been with Prudential for fifteen years, and she's working with a new employee to help her build relationships and a team to help support what needs to get done. "I have told her that her job responsibilities affect the organization, and she'll be more effective if she engages others to make decisions and execute on the objectives. I wouldn't be in the position I'm in today if I didn't know how to create relationships with the right

> *It's not what you know, it's who knows you know.*
>
> Jean M. Otte

75

people and to have them help me drive for the intended results."

At the end of 2008, a San Francisco Bay Area LEAD graduation group, Peer Team 7, consisting of Lesley Andrews from Intuit, Kim Lam from KLA-Tencor, and Dev Patel from Cisco Systems, created the following ten tips in finding a mentor or establishing a network (more on mentoring in chapter 9).

1. Time to Get Started. The fiscal year has ended and you are writing your performance goals. Now is the perfect time to formulate career and development goals. Who will be your learning partner on your FY09 mentoring odyssey?

2. Who Should it Be? You can't start a mentoring relationship without asking someone to be your mentor. Find a mentoring partner who can challenge your thinking, ask tough questions, and listen well. Seek out high-performing individuals who take an interest in your development. Commit to a set period of time prior to starting. Think about multiple mentors. It could be your personal board of directors.

3. Build the Relationship. Identify common interests that bridge to relationships. Establishing a meaningful human connection and building the relationship are the foundations for building effective mentoring partnerships. Keep trust levels high through confidentiality.

4. What Do You Want to Learn? Make sure you and your mentoring partner(s) understand, define, and agree to the learning goals of the mentoring relationship. Brainstorm a list of learning opportunities with your mentoring partner when you begin your mentoring. Establish objective measures to gauge success.

5. Connection is Key. Establish points of connection early on in the relationship. Be sensitive to the day-to-day needs of your mentoring partner while identifying multiple venues for communication that work for you both. Set a regular contact schedule and be flexible. Continually check on the effectiveness of the partnership.

6. Location, Location, Location. Even long distance mentoring is possible through effective communication. A quick e-mail, an instant message, or a very short conversation can work on an ongoing basis. At other points, longer conversations or exchanges take place. Knowing which to use and when is advantageous.

7. Write it Down. Keeping a journal or log is one way to add depth to your learning. Regularly set aside time to write about your experiences. As you describe your learning, consider what happened and what was really going on.

8. Be prepared. Keep an ongoing list of questions and needs to discuss when you meet. Be open to

feedback and the discussion to understand what it means. Be willing to try new things and to take risks.

9. Assess How It's Going. Mentoring relationships that are proactive and continuously work at evaluating their relationship are more likely to stay on course and to achieve their learning goals than those that do not. The evaluation conversation should become an established part of the mentoring relationship. It can be a simple conversation that answers the question, "how are we doing?" Or it can be a more in-depth conversation in which partners assess (a) the relationship, (b) the learning process, and (c) gauging process in achieving goals.

10. Do Your Homework. Mentoring requires no less than careful preparation of the mentoring partners. When self-preparation is ignored, more often than not, the results are dissatisfaction with the outcome or derailment of the relationship. You will want to reflect on your purpose, be clear about goals and objectives, and be willing to candidly share your needs, expectations, and limits.

By following the above list, you will help align yourself properly with the right people. A mentoring relationship should benefit all of the people in the relationship.

SUMMARY:

Successful Leaders...

1. Create a network of strategic alliances, internally and externally, to assist them in broadening their business perspectives.

2. Establish a diverse "Board of Directors " to assist them in their ongoing development.

3. Examine how they see and interact with others.

4. Seek out mentors at all levels to assist them with their ongoing development and goals.

5. Ask for help to assist with their goals and objectives.

6. Offer help to others to assist them with their goals and objectives.

7. Seek out opportunities to demonstrate their competence.

CALL TO ACTION:

●Assess the members of your "board of directors" to determine how well they are serving your needs. Create the best board to support your business and development needs today—and review its composition periodically.

●Identify the critical decision makers in your organization and determine what they know about you. Create a plan to ensure they know what they need to know about you.

●Identify a crucial associate to mentor. Set up a meeting with him/her over the next month. Periodically, assess the mentoring relationship by asking your mentee for feedback on your mentoring skills, such as what you do/provide that is helpful, and what could you do differently.

NOTES

NOTES

Rule #4:
Manage Work,
Lead People

One of the keys to effective leadership is the "softer skills" or having a high degree of E.Q., (emotional intelligence quotient) as well as I.Q (intelligence quotient). "Women possess these skills in abundance," says Rosina. "They just need to learn how to leverage them into strengths." This is one thing that women in all the WUI programs hear. "Women are so used to being highly competent and valued for doing tangible things," Rosina says. "But when they move into positions of leadership, they then have to define the work and ask themselves, 'How do I lead others in the things I used to do?'"

> *Leading people demands active participation. The skill cannot be learned from watching from the sidelines.*
>
> Timothy Warneka

In order to do this, a leader must provide a clear vision for the department and staff, and also provide the context of why the work is important for the department and the company. The leader must help everyone see the vision of where they are going, and then foster an alignment for greater impact for the employees, department, and the company.

What is the one thing that every successful leader has in common? When we ask this question in our programs we hear a wide variety of adjectives, including competence, confidence, integrity, and many more. What we, at WUI, believe is that one thing every leader has in common is: followers. And followers are led. But too often managers try to manage people, when they should be managing processing and leading their people.

The most important role of a leader is to create and support an inclusive environment in which people want to contribute, where they are trained and empowered to do so, and where they feel they are valued as an integral part to the success of the company. Employees also want to be recognized and rewarded for their contributions. And it is the leader's primary function to help others to produce the needed results.

The leader truly must "walk the talk". Nothing is more discouraging than to observe a leader who is not a role model for his or her employees. Leaders must model the behaviors they expect to see in others. Leaders also need to be approachable and respected, rather than feared, especially since fear doesn't bring out people's best.

Leaders know they don't have to know it all or have all of the answers. They do know how to get those answers, and highly successful leaders surround themselves with diverse alliances that can provide perspectives and expertise in order for the leaders to make smart decisions. Leaders also know how to ask great questions and then actively listen to the feedback they are given. They are respectful and grateful for feedback, even if they don't agree with it, and they give feedback to others that helps them improve and grow. Instead of trying to be superwomen, doing everything themselves, leaders know to win at the game of business, it takes a team effort.

Have you ever stopped to consider how selfish it is to do everything yourself? Women have a tendency to take on all of the work and to accomplish every task themselves, because it is often easier to do things this way. We think it saves time, hassle, etc. But Rosina reminds WUI participants that doing everything by yourself is selfish. As leaders, we have to give others space and opportunity to develop. Others need time to learn and grow, and your role as a leader is to nurture other people. Jean calls that enriching the soil in the garden so that the flowers (your colleagues and employees) can blossom. And a WUI mentor reminds us that part of encouraging people to grow is realizing that people may perform tasks differently than we do, so it is best to focus on the outcome, not on the process used to undertake the task.

Feedback and communication skills are imperative in doing this. Yet many women aren't quite sure how to give appropriate and adequate feedback. Most people instinctively interpret feedback as telling people what they are doing wrong or what they need to do differently. To be effective leaders we need to provide specific feedback on what is being done well and on what needs to be developed further. Good leaders know that telling people what they are doing well is vital so that they are encouraged to continue doing it. A secret that great leaders know is to not only let people know what they are seeing a person do well, but then to spend time discussing why it was so valuable—to the manager, to the job, and to the organization. For it to be effective the feedback should describe what was done and how it impacted the department or company. Most of the time people know if what they are doing meets the standards or expectations. Constructive feedback needs to provide an opportunity for an employee to grow and develop.

We focus at WUI on how to give constructive feedback so people don't feel attacked. And in order for someone not to feel attacked, you have to focus on the task, not on the person, so that the next time the task is done, it can be done more effectively. As a leader, you cannot be successful without the people around you being successful as well, so you need to acknowledge their successes.

DON'T BE "CUELESS"

You also cannot be successful without accurately reading cues. Every environment/situation/person gives off cues as to what is going on. Some are very obvious. Others are extremely subtle. It is vital to look for cues and to become highly aware of the cues around us. Many successful leaders have a very high degree of cue consciousness, which they have honed over time. One of the ways in which to check how you measure up in this area (being cue-conscious as opposed to cueless) is to think about how often you are surprised by what happens. Sometimes the surprise is due to us not properly identifying the cues around us.

We ask women in our programs to assess their skill in this area, and we ask how they might go about improving in this area. We recommend, first and foremost, to use your mentors, trusted colleagues, and bosses to give their perspectives on a situation about which you are concerned or that you are not confident you are reading well. We encourage women to do a post-mortem after a meeting to check out their perceptions and observations with others who attended the same meeting, as this is a great way to determine their powers of observation. Since many meetings are now held virtually, the need to pick up on cues is of uttermost importance.

What are some of the cues to listen for in a virtual meeting? One of the most significant cues is lack of comments or questions by the participants in the meeting. A "check in" can be conducted to make sure everyone is engaged. WUI recommends that if you are leading a virtual meeting, take time at the conclusion of the meeting to ask each attendee to answer the question, "What questions do you have, and what was valuable for you to hear?"

But some cues are not specifically silence or comments about business-related issues. Most people have been raised not to discuss politics or religion, especially at the office. However, it is important to be sure you are cue conscious about what and how you discuss every topic in the workplace. One example Jean shares is how she often observed women in the workplace who were quite vocal in front of their colleagues about not being interested in sports. Given the fact that the vast majority of males (and increasing numbers of females) will start off the week with conversations about weekend sports, stating loudly your lack of interest in sports is truly cueless. This kind of statement excludes the person from networking opportunities and potential strategic alliances that they could have established by expressing an interest.

Another key to successful leadership is to recognize that timing is everything. A cue conscious leader does not give the "right message at the wrong time". A leader looks for cues when approaching people and asking for their time. A leader knows not to interrupt when the person is working on a priority issue or dealing with a budget. A good leader respects people's time, and checks in with them on a regular basis to see what they need.

PROVIDE OPPORTUNITIES
FOR OTHERS TO GROW

Angela Szymusiak, Senior Manager, Engagement, at Adobe Systems, and a 2000 TEAM graduate, says that early in her career she tried to do a lot to protect those on her team, and unfortunately that didn't give them the opportunity to grow and stretch. Instead of protecting your people, she says, "You need to be willing to take the risk, to ask the right questions, and then stay out of the kitchen. Give people opportunities that give them the chance to shine."

Linda Neuman, M.D., M.B.A., MSL, Regional Director of Millennium Pharmaceuticals, agrees. When she put on several teleconferences she gave a colleague an opportunity to do one. "I was behind the scenes in case she needed assistance," Dr. Neuman advises. "And even though it takes more work to coach people and to help instill confidence within them, it is an important experience so they can go do the work on their own later."

She further states that when managers don't provide opportunities or delegate to others, it can make them look weak. She gave an example of when one of her team members was supposed to give a presentation and then became ill. "I asked for a volunteer, since I was the team leader, but no one volunteered, so I just figured I'd do it myself. Because I didn't delegate, it made me look like a weak leader, and I took the opportunity for growth away from someone else. I realized this at WUI. Next time, I will ask for volunteers and if no one does, I will assign the task."

Szymusiak recounts that back when she was a direct people manager (after eighteen years at Adobe, she manages projects now, not people), one woman on her team with experience in college recruiting and diversity wanted more breadth of expertise in other Human Resources areas. Adobe encourages all of its employees to create individual development plans so Szymusiak talked with her team member about her IDP and discussed what could be done. Then she arranged for the woman to sit in on the compensation team's weekly staff meetings for a whole quarter so she could learn about compensation (i.e. what were the key challenges, how were

> A leader takes people where they want to go. A great leader takes people where they don't necessarily want to go but where they ought to be.
>
> Rosalynn Carter

92

issues being resolved, what kind of skills were needed for that team, what the jobs entailed, etc.). "I
learned a tremendous amount and built relationships
on the team," Szymusiak recalls. "The next quarter a
compensation analyst position opened up and
because of her newly acquired knowledge and relationships, she got the job."

Dr. Neuman stresses there is a difference between
helping people grow personally vs. developing job-
specific skills. "If I had my druthers everyone I led
would get promoted above me. A good leader
develops people to the next level." She adds that
another way to get people recognized and promoted to the next level is "by tooting their team members' horns." She says, "A lot of managers aren't
good at self promotion or communicating the
accomplishments of their people. Individually and
collectively this needs to be done more, as it builds
trust, relationships, and careers."

Szymusiak wants her team to be seen as subject
matter experts, whenever possible. She wants them
to be the people up front, even if they are usually in
the trenches doing the tough work. "When I've been
a team leader and had to speak to the executive
team," she says, "I usually brought someone on my
team to shadow me, so that they could learn how to
successfully navigate presenting to the executives by
watching and listening."

GIVE AND RECEIVE EFFECTIVE FEEDBACK

Another part of building trust involves the way a leader handles giving and receiving feedback. Executive Development Consultant, Master Certified Coach, and author Val Williams writes in her book *Get the Best Out of Your People and Yourself* (2002) that feedback needs to be immediate, specific, and face-to-face (whenever possible.) Szymusiak says, "Adobe sees feedback as a gift. This is why we have a quarterly and an annual review process and encourage our managers to give feedback on an ongoing basis." No one can get better without feedback. The feedback process at Adobe looks at what was done and how it aligns with the company's core values. "People need to understand the reasoning behind the feedback," says Szymusiak. "If it was good, what was good about it? And make sure it is honest opinion, not flattery."

Williams says that "feedback is observed behavior, not the manager's interpretation... Feedback is like the instrument readings that help an airplane stay on course. As a manager, you should go out of your way to deliver positive feedback, even on small items. This is what will balance the stage for the times when you have to give negative feedback."

Feedback doesn't always have to come from the top down. Szymusiak says Adobe cultivates an environment where people feel valued and recognized, where handwritten notes or a small gift mean a lot. "Personalized recognition is the key," she says. "Match the person's interests with how you are rewarding them in public. One of the best gifts of positive feedback I received was a CD of music from my favorite artist. My manager knew it was a thank-you gift I would really appreciate."

Dr. Neuman advises to ask a person's permission if you are providing him or her with feedback, especially if the person is higher up the feeding chain than you are. "Feedback develops good relationships if it is given in the right setting," she says. "Provide praise in public and critical evaluations in private." It is important that both the employee and senior management hear what the employee did well and why it exceeded expectations. However, corrective comments are best discussed without an audience larger than one."

With regard to managing work, Dr Newman adds, "Prioritization and delegation are the most important elements. We must assess the importance and deadlines associated with each project to determine how much time and when the tasks should be tackled. Other considerations should be given to the level of detail required to complete the job. Many people get stuck in the weeds and do not understand the concept of 'good enough'. When it comes to delegation, the least qualified person should be the one to do the work. For example, while the VP of medical affairs is qualified to do a managed care presentation, that level of expertise is not necessary."

HOW CAN YOU IDENTIFY A LEADER?

One main difference between a manager and a leader is that a leader has a vision that she or he can easily translate for others to see. And this vision is usually something people want to embrace and be an integral part of.

Leaders also initiate and implement ideas. Leaders are results-oriented, and as we say at WUI, "results are not a gender issue." Leaders also seek out opportunities to contribute, especially in more difficult or challenging times. Take a moment to think about your work environment during the last year or so—these have not been stable times for the United States. Think about the people who have shone in your company. What made them do so? Often we think they are savvy business people, when the truth is, they probably have highly tuned powers of observation and are cue conscious. They notice things others don't.

All effective leaders also continuously demonstrate a desire to learn and to improve their skills. American businessman and utilities expert Henry L.

Doherty said once, "Get over the idea that only children should spend their time in study. Be a student as long as you still have something to learn, and this means all your life."

SUMMARY:

Successful Leaders:

1. Establish and communicate a clear vision.

2. Are innovative—they focus on and achieve results.

3. Are attuned to the organization's values and cues.

4. Make things happen through and with others.

5. Create an inclusive environment to foster the development of others.

6. Seek out feedback on their performance and contributions.

CALL TO ACTION:

●Assess the quality of the feedback you provide your staff and colleagues. Identify how they demonstrate their understanding of your vision. Determine if there are gaps in understanding and create a plan to have a greater alignment.

●Evaluate your effectiveness in communicating across the organization—especially with those whose style/focus varies from yours. Identify key strategies to integrate into your communication strategy that will increase your effectiveness and build stronger relationships.

●Identify one person who presents the greatest challenge to you at work and set up a meeting with him/her to learn more about his/her perspective. Determine what you can do to improve the relationship.

NOTES

NOTES

OTTE · RACIOPPI · FERGUSON

NOTES

Rule #5:
Look Like a Leader

Rosina asks the question: stop and think for a moment: what do you think a leader should look like? How do the leaders you admire appear in public? When we talk about looking like a leader we are discussing overall presence—everything from workspace and appearance to language, grammar, and body language. All of these combine to help other people form impressions of you, and these impressions cause judgments to be made that then get translated into whether you look like a leader, or not.

Being powerful is like being a lady. If you have to tell people you are, you aren't.

Margaret Thatcher

When you are meeting with others in your organization, what are their initial reactions to you? Because you never get a second chance to make a first impression, how you introduce yourself, what you contribute to a conversation, and how you look are very important. Think for a moment, how often have you based your opinion of someone on what you thought when you first met him or her?

YOUR WORK SPACE SHOULD
SHOWCASE LEADERSHIP

Now think about your workspace. If a co-worker or supervisor you haven't met yet walked into your office or cubicle, what would be her first thoughts about your space? Does it say, "This person manages work well and could possibly use more responsibility," or does your workspace scream, "Help! I'm already overwhelmed with work. I can't take on any more."

Think about how you feel when first visiting a colleague's/customer's/client's workspace. What do you first notice? What are your expectations of that space? We all want to show some personality in our cubicles or offices. That might mean displaying your sense of humor or showing off your family or pets through photos. Or maybe you want to display something that is near and dear to your heart, something that you believe helps identify you as more than just an employee. Our workspaces, just like our home environments, reflect who we are as people. Diplomas or awards, things that identify our capabilities and accomplishments should be displayed.

The problem, Jean says, is when the things in our workplace become a detraction of or a distraction from our work. "It doesn't speak highly of our leadership skills to have a shelf full of collectibles. Your workspace shouldn't be cluttered and it should look professional. Clearly display that you are organized and that you can quickly locate and retrieve data." You should be conscious of what you consider appealing, as things that we find cute or humorous may not be seen that way by all of our co-workers. Don't alienate yourself from colleagues by what you have in your office.

Of course we all have times when we are swamped with deadlines and projects and our workspace looks like a gale-force wind has blown through it. If you are faced with clutter or piles of papers and general mess, but you have to meet with colleagues, clients, customers, corporate executives or even potential employees, Jean recommends holding your meeting in the conference room. This way, the person(s) with whom you are meeting won't be distracted by your mess and you will still look like a professional.

TALK, PLAN, AND PROJECT LIKE A LEADER

Another part of presence is how you talk, both in what you say and how you present information. Do you think about what you say before you go to meetings? Do you have a strategy for each meeting you attend? How do you position yourself and what should your colleagues know about the issue being discussed? You need to go into every meeting knowing what you plan to contribute. And then you need to speak in a clear, concise, and business-like fashion. Many women wait until everyone else has had a say during the meeting. This tactic doesn't make you look like a leader. Pat Kirkland, CEO of Skills to Success International, tells women in the LEAD program that "powerful people take up time and take up space."

Amy Gonzales, Regional Director of West Coast Operations for WOMEN Unlimited, explains, "For women, this means standing with your feet apart at hip distance and your shoulders and head straight. One of the hardest things for women to practice is to simply stand still, with no fidgeting, swaying, head tilts, etc."

Gonzales says that since much of our time is spent sitting in meetings we need to also be aware of our body posture at the conference table. "One of the women in LEAD was a senior manager in engineering and all of her male peers had director titles. She was constantly frustrated that she did not have the title she felt she deserved, and she also didn't feel her colleagues gave her equal time at weekly staff meetings. After coaching her, we realized that her posture at the meeting table appeared deferential— she sat primly in her chair, made sure her papers were neatly organized in front of her, clasped her hands in her lap, and she nodded her head a lot while others were talking. After we worked on her taking up more space at the table and assuming a more casual, asymmetrical posture in her chair by opening her arms and spreading out her things in front of her, she reported back the next month that she was being paid attention to. And two months later, she was promoted to director."

In the 1989 book *You Are the Message* by Roger Ailes and Jon Krausher, the authors write, "When you communicate with someone, it's not just the words you choose to send to the other person that make up the message. You're also sending signals about what kind of person you are—by your eyes, your facial expression, your body movement, your vocal pitch, tone, volume, and intensity..."

Even though your words account for only a part of the message, Rosina encourages women to strategically plan what to say before the meeting. "Laser your speech," she says. "Make your speech high level and high impact. If people need more information they will ask you a question. Don't be a fire hose dousing or drowning people with your message." Dr. Linda Neuman says that when she speaks, "The bottom line is first. In e-mails and in leaving voice mail messages, this is extremely important: be succinct. Saying 'I think' or 'I believe' does not make you look or sound confident. And don't always be

OTTE · RACIOPPI · FERGUSON

the first person to speak. Hear a few comments and then make a comment of your own, especially if you are on a job interview."

Victoria M. Pratt, Ph.D., FACMG, Chief Director, Molecular Genetics, at the Nichols Institute at Quest Diagnostics, seconds this advice. "When we speak in front of the FDA and other government agencies, we have to convey our message in a simple, direct manner, lasering in on the crux of the message. I help others prepare their presentations and I tell them to state the argument, the 'this is this' and then quickly list the reasons why. Be factual and concise."

Another piece of speaking like a leader is to pay attention to your voice inflections. Professor and author Deborah Tannen has devoted her life's work to studying communication patterns and differences between males and females. One thing she notes is that women often speak with an upward inflection at the end of their sentences. This means their voices pitch higher at the end of the sentence than it does at the beginning or middle of the sentence, making statements often sound like questions.

Gonzales says, "Simply putting a downward inflection—a mental period—at the end of each statement will make others hear you as more confident versus tentative sounding," In WOMEN Unlimited programs, adds Gonzales, "We practice the downward inflections by playing an improvisational game whereby each woman gets to be the expert on a nonsensical topic. For example, one person will explain to a group why turkey vultures love to line dance. That person has to sound like a confident leader—through their voice inflections, cadence, and rhythm why this nonsensical thing is 'true'."

One thing that WUI teaches is that leaders focus on results, not on activities. How much of your talk is centered on how much you do, how much time it took or how hard you worked? "Check your pre-sentations, your status updates, your e-mail commu-nications," Gonzales advises. "Do they talk about activities or focus on results? And when you talk about your results, make sure to tie them into the goals of the organization. This is part of how you sound and look like a leader."

Additionally, Dr. Neuman stresses how not only what you say is important but how some positions in a room are more beneficial than others. "In the meeting room, most people believe the best place to sit in a meeting is at the ends of the table, but the power position is in the middle of the table facing the door. This way you get a full view of the room, never have your back to anyone entering the room, and are in the best position for making eye contact with participants. You can maximize your advan-tage and influence simply by where you sit in a meeting room."

And this can be one of the greatest challenges for

women because, depending on the industry, women may not have role models. Many times women are so caught up in producing quality work, they may not think about how they present themselves in the way they talk or dress.

DRESS LIKE A LEADER

The key to dressing like a leader is to attire yourself for the level of job that you want, not the level you are in. This is true no matter what industry you work in, and each work place has its unique "uniform", from very formal to very casual, depending on the industry. In order to look like a leader, you must dress like a leader, and "look like a leader who is ready to play the game," says Jean. And in the times of casual office dress, for men this usually means a polo style shirt and khakis with tennis shoes or Docksiders. But for women, the choices are mind-boggling. So how do you dress casually and still look like a leader, as opposed to someone headed to the beach, in an outfit that shows too much skin?

Rosina stresses that we don't all need to go back to the 1970s and 1980s, when women in business tried to dress like men, with power suits that were far from feminine. Women can dress in ways that are business-like, comfortable, and womanly and still look like leaders. But noisy shoes and excessive jewelry can be distracting. So can brightly colored nails or fingernails embedded with gemstones. What message are you trying to send in your choice of clothes, shoes, and accessories? Will the articles you choose help you or hurt you?

Years ago when Maria Shriver was on the nightly news, the station was inundated with calls one night because she appeared with her hair in tiny braids all over her head. She had just come back from vacation with her husband and kids, and she and her daughters had their hair braided like the locals. The phone calls were from viewers who didn't think she looked "professional."

Think about your wardrobe. What are your favorite outfits to wear at work? Gonzales states, "It's time for hard truth. If you haven't changed anything in your wardrobe or your hairstyle for more than five years, there is a good chance you will be seen as not current or up-to-date in your thoughts and ideas as well. This doesn't mean to dress younger than you are, it means staying current in your appearance. One of our mentors puts it this way: Dress as if you are on a job interview every day because in reality, you are."

When you think about your clothes, also determine how functional they are for your job. Dr. Pratt says that when she is working in the lab she wears a nice sweater and wool pants, with her lab coat. A business suit would be out of place and impractical, plus it might not be safe. "For safety issues, we wear lab coats, closed-toe shoes, and nothing too short," she says. "I have sent people home to change clothes if their attire was not appropriate."

Dr. Pratt recalls, "When I was in grad school, that's the first time I had to think about my attire. I was wearing a khaki skirt that came to my knees and a nice coordinating shirt, and a woman doctor told me I was dressed inappropriately to see patients because I didn't have on pantyhose. She basically told me I wasn't dressed like a leader."

Another WUI participant had a similar experience. She looked very young, even though she was a scientist in her thirties. But she appeared younger because she wore her hair long and straight and pulled back into a ponytail on most days. Her attire still screamed "college years", and because of this, she wasn't seen as a strong leader by her peers or by her company's management. When she attended a WUI program, she realized she needed to update her look so she cut her hair and bought some new business outfits that were versatile, chic, and still fit her scientific corporate culture. Her colleagues almost immediately started taking her more seriously.

Manage your presence with how you look and how you sound, and when you do, you will demonstrate confidence in your abilities and people will see you are high performing and have high potential. As Gonzales points out, "The good news is that you get to decide how you want to be seen and heard as a leader; it's the choices you make each day, in every meeting and in each interaction with peers and management." You can decide how you are seen by others in your company.

SUMMARY:

Successful Leaders...

1. Have a presence that inspires confidence.

2. Are role models for aspiring leaders.

3. Communicate in an articulate and impactful manner.

4. Communicate effectively with all levels of the organization.

5. Have a professional appearance (clothes, accessories, hairstyle) that represents effective leadership.

CALL TO ACTION:

●Assess the impact of your communication style. Determine whether you display confidence in your abilities and whether you suit up properly for the game.

●Assess whether your organizational presence supports your professional goals.

●Identify a crucial associate to meet with and gain greater insight about how you sound and look.

NOTES

NOTES

NOTES

Rule #6:
Think Excellence,
Not Perfection

As Rosina says, "Perfection is a word that shouldn't even be in our vocabularies." Pursue excellence in everything; do not pursue perfection. An issue that arises with many participants at WOMEN Unlimited is the tendency of women to over-deliver on an issue because they want it done perfectly. But in business the needs at hand need to be met, which many times means not reaching a level of perfection. To use the analogy of academic grades, in business that often means "B" and even "C" level work is perfectly acceptable and even warranted. Excellence and perfection are not the same thing. That bears repeating: excellence and perfection are not the same thing.

Never let the urgent crowd out the important.

Kelly Catlin Walker

Perfection is one of the key derailers for women; when encountering a situation or problem, women may fall into the trap of seeking the resolution that solves the problem AND provides an additional benefit. On the surface that should be a good thing—doing more than is asked or expected. But consider the additional amount of time and effort needed to accomplish the "extra benefit". How often do you do this? (For every situation? Half the situations?) You must think about how often you expend extra effort and whether it's beneficial to do so for every situation. The sad truth is that often the additional work and effort may not be noticed or valued. Others rarely value the extra time and the energy expended in pursuit of the perfect answer/resolution. And this extra time and energy expended typically has a negative impact as it causes others to have the perception that you do not clearly understand what is needed to resolve situations. (We will discuss this concept again in Chapter 8, the chapter on decision-making.)

Famous NFL coach Vince Lombardi once told his football players his vision and philosophy of teamwork: they would work hard and along the journey they would find excellence. Lombardi said, "Perfection is not attainable." Yet many women still search for perfection and this striving limits their careers. While striving for perfection it is hard to let stuff go, so you end up overworking and overdoing the process. This often leads to not understanding the projects, the customers, etc. The road to perfection causes some people to become so entrenched in the work that they miss the big picture.

Perfectionism is career limiting as it focuses on a task; completing it to a standard of perfectionism loses sight of the end goal. The end goal is how the task moves the organization's goals and objectives forward and impacts its external customers. The issue is compounded even further as many women grow increasingly frustrated when all of their work is not appreciated. This creates a vicious cycle: doing more work than may be needed and then being disappointed that that work is not appreciated.

Rosina often asks women in our programs, "How do you serve your customer?" When she worked in the chemical industry, the president Rosina worked for would ask her how she served the customer. "As head of HR, I was in a staff role, and at first I could identify a few areas where I impacted our external customers. His question caused me to realize that in order to provide excellent support for the organization, I needed to ensure that my department was focused on how the programs and initiatives we offered impacted our customers. This new focus helped me identify the areas that needed my attention, as well as which areas could wait," Rosina explains.

Staying focused on the business impact and the customer provides clarity and ensures that the end product delivers a solution that serves both constituents. Staying focused on delivering what the customer needs—not more or less—ensures that your customers will be pleased and you will break the cycle from delivering more than is needed.

All of our business decisions and work require excellence, but in most industries, few decisions or work require perfection. But many people, women especially, do not comprehend the difference. A lot of women's work goes unnoticed and is undervalued because it doesn't meet the needs of the issues at hand. It may be "beautiful" but not timely.

Susan Kendrick, Regional Director of WOMEN Unlimited's Southern Region, relates this story on the subject of perfectionism. "Tom, the vice president of a national sales team, confided in me and asked for my help. It seemed that his direct report, a director of a sales team, who was a wonderfully dedicated, key contributor, suffered from perfectionism and it was impacting not only his team but his customers as well.

'The thing I need Pam to understand is that there are times when I don't need 100% of the information,' he said. 'We recently had a customer issue that didn't go well. In an effort to remedy the situation, I asked Pam to provide me with the details. Five days later I still didn't have the report that I needed in order to rectify the problem. Pam was still adding to her report and the customer was still waiting for us to make it right.'"

Kendrick explains, "Perfectionism is often a behavior that is learned from those who raised us. I have many examples but one that has remained with me for years is one of a brilliant young participant, a scientist who worked at a pharmaceutical company. At a young age she learned the value of perfection. She explained that every time she brought home a paper with an 'A' on it, her father would scold and ask, "Didn't they give you a chance for extra credit?" This type of ingrained perfectionist expectation and subsequent behavior—striving to meet the perfectionist standards of our parents—is very hard to overcome, but it can be done."

Think of the times in your life when you have over-delivered. What caused you to do that? Jill had an adult student who worked as a Sales Manager a few years ago take her Women in Management class. The woman was the classic Type-A personality over-achiever. For every writing assignment she turned in twice the number of pages as was necessary. While Jill appreciated her effort, she didn't appreciate that the student kept asking for time extensions and for her to review drafts of the papers. The student was so obsessed with perfection that it almost paralyzed her as a functional student and contributor to the class. American author and journalist Anne Quindlen says, "The thing that is really hard, and really amazing, is giving up on being perfect and beginning the work of becoming yourself."

In order to overcome these behavior patterns and to work on becoming your "imperfect self", Kendrick recommends first recognizing that the business world is not run like the academic world. "As children we are driven by grades and measured against those A's. That same method is not applied to our business world, except for in a handful of careers where precision is critical, such as brain surgery or with Sarbanes Oxley certified account-ants. It is not realistic for the majority of us and the perfectionist mindset is not warranted.

"Perfectionists are afraid of failure, but a strong leader is shaped by her failures and experiences."

Kendrick offers these simple solutions and strate-gies to pull out of the perils of perfectionism:

- Put out a 'rough' draft and ask, "What's still miss-ing that the recipient needs?" This strategy is espe-cially helpful for perfectionists because they can always add more and make it better. By labeling your document a 'draft', you are allowing yourself to let go before you have all of the details buttoned down. It affords you the opportunity to add more if others tell you that they need it.

- Put time limitations and boundaries for your end product/deliverable. Many senior management posi-tions require that you stay high level in your actions and thinking and not get mired down in the details, which perfectionists often do. Concentrate on the end goal and what will yield the greatest results. Use the 10-10-10 rule. How much will it matter in ten minutes? Ten days? Ten months? Ten years?

• Enlist the help of a crucial associate who knows you do great work and who can help you move past your perfectionism tendencies. Ask him or her to review your work thus far and tell you what, if anything, is missing.

• Experiment with lower standards to see that they work. Start with a low risk opportunity. Perhaps in putting together a slide deck for your weekly meeting, create eighty percent of what you typically would have in the slide deck and see if there is any negative impact.

• Learn to ask questions to understand the scope of what is needed. Great questions include: How much detail do you need? Who will be using this information? Will there be an opportunity to add to this project?

• Finally, admit that it's scary to fail and that you are going to from time to time! We are all shaped by our failures and what we learn from them. So challenge yourself to get over your assumptions about needing to be perfect. Ask yourself, "What's the worst thing that can happen if this isn't perfect?"

PERFECTIONISM = WORKAHOLISM

United Airline's HR Business Partner Gina Flaig,

LEAD program alum, echoes some of these same sentiments about the dangers of perfectionism when she related her most life-changing experiences in the WUI program. "I actually went into the LEAD program wanting to be a perfect participant, which is kind of ironic. The most meaningful session for me was the one around balance because I didn't have any. We discussed the book *Coming Up for Air: How to Build a Balanced Life in a Workaholic World*, by Beth Sawi, and I realized how I had completely lost touch with what my priorities were, and I was certainly not honoring them. I had systematically discontinued most of my personal relationships and was letting my work life take over. At work, difficult things were going on, including death of a colleague, layoffs, and reorganizations. I had come to the awareness that I was [the] only one who could take control of my life and that the time was now. With the support of the WUI group and of many others, I decided to make some changes.

> *The real secret of joy in work is contained in one word—Excellence. To know how to do something well is to enjoy it.*
>
> Pearl S. Buck

"I had to consider things like, if I wasn't there to answer the phone at 8 P.M., or to return e-mail at 2 A.M., what would people think of me? But I started to make changes and I learned that my performance wasn't negatively impacted at all. In fact, people regarded me more as a thought partner instead of a convenient resource. They asked for my opinions and input. I was a classic over-deliverer. I didn't stop with what people needed. I'd provide add-ons and come up with unnecessary self-imposed deadlines with what people didn't really want or need, and I ultimately wasted my time on non-valued added work. And it didn't serve any business purpose. It was risky for me to not always be the one available. I moved from being so focused on thinking I needed to build daily a strong reputation and performance track record, and I realized I already had them in place. So I could spend my time on other things to better contribute to the company and to my development. But we were taught at WUI not to work for the gold star, as our businesses aren't giving them out. I'm more mindful of this now. Sure, I still have that 'good girl' mantra in my head; yet, I try to quiet that voice and listen for the 'smart girl'.

"My performance continues to be strong. And since WUI I have remained committed to my personal priorities. I have since gotten married and had kids, gained professional experience at other companies, and gotten promoted a few times. Recently, I was offered a role that I knew would not allow me to honor my personal nor professional priorities, and I had the courage to make the decision that was right for me. My life has more balance, and I'm much more flexible with myself and with others. I played it too safe before, but now I take risks, make mistakes, and my colleagues see me as more courageous, an asset that I am proud of."

THE DANGERS OF MULTI-TASKING

The ability to multi-task can be viewed as a strength—and in some situations it is. When needing to complete several tasks in a short amount of time, being able to multi-task is essential. As a leader, multi-tasking can be a trap that needs to be avoided as it can cause us to become distracted from the main goals. Rosina explains, "I have seen women in a blur of activity, very focused on getting everything done. It is crucial to identify the important items or activities to be completed now, and to avoid the temptation to complete more just because you have the ability. I often tell women, just because you can doesn't mean you should. Knowing when and where to focus your attention is the art of leadership!"

DON'T DO LIST VS. TO DO LIST

Another way to get yourself out of the perfectionism trap is to create a "don't do list". Jean says, "Many women attempt to do far too much and are unrealistic about what they can achieve. When they don't get their 'to dos' accomplished they feel they have somehow failed to achieve what they should have been able to achieve." And sometimes trying to accomplish so much causes us to multitask, but we learn very quickly that when we multitask, while we are doing many things at once, we are rarely doing well those many things at once.

Jean says that by creating a "don't do list", women can examine what is essential versus what is not essential. "It's amazing how many 'not essentials' we have in our lives," Jean points out. "I like to ask myself this question: If this did not get done today what would happen? What if this task did not get done this week? Or this month? Or this year? If there are no consequences, do I really have to do it?"

SUMMARY:

Successful leaders...

1. Are committed to excellence, not perfection.

2. Establish/negotiate realistic timelines for deliverables.

3. Are flexible and adaptable to meet changing requirements.

4. Stay focused to achieve the required deliverable.

5. Don't over-deliver when it's not needed.

6. Ask for help.

OTTE · RACIOPPI · FERGUSON

CALL TO ACTION:

●List three ways you serve your internal and external customers. Review how you are meeting their needs and whether you deliver what is expected (or if you over-deliver).

●Assess your effectiveness in how your proposals, ideas, etc. address customer needs and/or have a positive impact on the organizational goals. Identify one key individual who can provide you with feedback. Request that they provide you with their assessment of how effective you are.

●Start a Don't Do List. Review it each day to stay on track.

NOTES

NOTES

Rule #7:
Play Well With Others

The comments of the sixty-five women and men that Catalyst interviewed for their study, the "Unwritten Rules: What You Don't Know Can Hurt Your Career", have been classified into two main categories: behaviors and/or actions that are helpful to advance and individual skills and characteristics the organization values when it comes to promotion opportunities. These two categories are then further broken down into eight subsections each, titled the "Top Unwritten Rules to Advancement". More than half of these rules deal with "playing well with others"—from being a good communicator, to working well with others, to being communal, to understanding how to network and build relationships.

The key to successful leadership is influence, not authority.

Ken Blanchard

Rosina reminds WOMEN Unlimited participants, "People are people first, and then they are technically competent employees." Engaging people personally will cause them to want to engage with you professionally. Think about your male colleagues for a moment. They play hard together, but they also work hard together. They do this so the work doesn't feel like drudgery. When was the last time you connected with a co-worker like that?

Some people prefer to go to work and focus on the work itself and then go home; they rarely connect with the colleagues around them. A true leader does not just do the work but engages others in the process. A leader is not only approachable but also establishes and maintains connections with others in her company and in her industry. This helps the leader leverage people's skills and makes it easier to bring people together on projects—ensuring everyone's success.

When Jean was a young schoolgirl, she says she learned one of the most important lessons that has helped her throughout her life. When she got her report card her teacher added the comment, "one of Jean's attributes is that she plays well with others". Jean believes that no matter how smart or accomplished a person may be, the ability to interact with others in the workplace and to make others feel valued is the key to getting things accomplished. So often, despite skills in many areas, people do not appreciate that the way to get things done is through and with others.

Often times when we observe people in leadership

positions, they give off a message that they know what's best and that they do not need others' opinions or perspectives. This does not motivate others to want to help or point out potential problems. Jean remembers a time when she observed first-hand a leader who had made the statement, "I don't care what people think about me. I'm here to get things done, not to win a Miss Congeniality contest." What this leader did not appreciate was that employees who could have pointed out the problems with a process that she was insisting be implemented decided they wouldn't bother. So they let the leader's decision result in failure. Clearly there was fault on both sides, since the employees let their actions (or inaction) cause a problem for the company. But even if the leader didn't want to play well with others, the employees should still try.

IT ISN'T PERSONAL; IT'S BUSINESS

One of the challenges for women in business is that we take things too personally. When we make a suggestion and it is challenged, or worse yet, dismissed, women become hurt and angry with the offender. For some women, when their ideas are not liked, this is interpreted as them not being liked personally.

It is interesting that most men are so accustomed to

women taking things personally that when we don't, they are caught off guard. "I remember my first board meeting where I was presenting my proposal for the company's new benefit plan," Rosina recalls. "Soon after I began my presentation, the members of the board (all men) starting asking me questions, and they were somewhat argumentative. I quickly switched gears and began asking questions to better understand their concerns. When I better understood their concerns, I asked if they would permit me to attend next month's meeting with a revised proposal. I returned to my office feeling good about the meeting. Afterwards, the president came into my office very concerned about how I was feeling. He thought I would be upset, as they did not like my idea. I laughed to myself and then shared with him that they gave me a gift: they did not like my idea. They were not rude or disrespectful to me, and I knew that they would like my presentation next month."

For many women, they so closely define who they are with what they do. When someone dislikes their ideas or proposals, this becomes a personal hurt. And then this hurt carries with them into each encounter with the person(s) who offended them, and it interferes with their ability to develop good working relationships. We know that effective leaders know how to build strong relationships throughout their organizations, so how they feel about the individuals—whether they like them or not—is not a consideration.

Building teams can be difficult, especially if the team members haven't met in person (which is common in today's global businesses) or if they know nothing about one another. When this is the case, how do you establish a team vision and team buy-in? Strong leaders know to schedule some "connect time" into each meeting. This connect time can be started by singling a person out for his or her specific accomplishments, and by allowing people to share their perspectives and insights. Good leaders create a meeting atmosphere where people can be supportive of one another. Even in a tough or negative situation, a leader knows how to disagree without being disagreeable. And this starts by never putting down others, never saying, "That was a stupid way to look at it."

Jean says that when she attended her first board meeting as an officer of a company, she was the only woman present at the meeting and thought it would be a good learning experience. But she didn't exactly learn what she had expected. She relates, "As the meeting began, two of my male colleagues got into a loud and highly contentious argument about a project. I was stunned by the verbal attacks and the fact that no one in the meeting seemed to be as appalled as I was. Once this fight was ended by one of the men agreeing to 'think about it', the meeting went on. What was even more amazing to me was that the men seemed to have completely forgotten what had occurred, so much so that when the meeting ended, they actually high-fived each other and went out for drinks and dinner.

"The next day we resumed the meeting and one of the men agreed he had thought about what was proposed by his 'opponent' and was 'onboard with it'. This was truly a moment of my coming to terms with how neither of these men had taken it personally. They were both back in the game and ready to play for the good of the team."

At WUI we talk about what this situation would have been like between two women. And without exception, at our workshops the women respond with comments like "there's no way I would be able to make nice" the next day or "I would hold a grudge". Women tend to take things too personally and it can impact how we are perceived.

VALUING OTHERS' PERSPECTIVES

Rosina advises that a better way to play well with others is to say, "We all have different ways of looking at things. I've never thought of that perspective. What made you think of that idea (or solution)? Have you thought of these things...?" This is one

146

way to engage, recognize, and develop others. Women leaders seed for their futures by helping people, especially by helping other women, and by encouraging those around them to play well with their co-workers.

Velma Monteiro-Tribble, Chief Operating Officer and Assistant Treasurer of the Alcoa Foundation and graduate of the WUI FEW program, says that she looks at how she treats people and how she'd like to be treated. She also looks at how she can equalize the playing field for the people who work for her, saying she looks "at cognitive and affective domains and intestinal (or emotional) fortitude." She asks herself and others, "What is your synchronicity? What is your inner spiritual being and how you feel about yourself and how you feel in your space? If all of that is right, fair, honest, with an air of competency and an air of respect, if you reach back and help others and make sure they are moving the same way, that is how you play well with others."

Monteiro-Tribble says she tries to stay in the background and cultivate others, their leadership, and their abilities. "Sometimes being fair and cultivating leadership isn't always what others want you to do. The bottom line is push, tug, and get people to do things. This is what people believe, but I believe that isn't where work productivity comes [from]," she says. "How much do you believe in cultivating others and how far will you go in doing this? You must take the risk to nurture others." She points out that it is easy to be in the front and take the honor, but the most honorable thing to do is to reach back and put others in the limelight.

Monteiro-Tribble recently did this when she was asked to speak at a gala in New York City, but she instead asked a staff person to give the presentation. "One of my assistants did it and it was an incredible night." But in order to do this, you have to help people prepare and be ready so they aren't embarrassed when the opportunities come. You must mentor people and prepare people in a way that isn't in anyone's job description. But this preparing others should be work you believe in, even if it is against the grain of what you've been taught previously.

The art of leadership is the act of getting someone else to do something you want done because he wants to do it.

Dwight D. Eisenhower

"One of the neat things in going through the FEW program is that I got to realize what I believed in is true, and I could confidently talk about these things and get validation that I was right. This is especially important for women. You can't be insecure when cultivating leadership.

"You need to strive to create other leaders every

day when you walk through the door," Monteiro-Tribble explains. And that is because as you move up the corporate ladder your success depends less on your own work and more on your ability to influence others. The greater your scope of responsibility the more you need the help of others to accomplish your objectives.

BE INFLUENTIAL IN YOUR ACTIONS

Deb Hornell, Midwest Regional Director of WOMEN Unlimited, says that many women in the WUI programs ask what it means to influence, and they want to know how to do it effectively. "Influence, negotiation, and conflict are often used interchangeably, when in fact, they are different aspects of achieving results through others. WOMEN Unlimited defines influence as 'the power to indirectly or intangibly affect a person or event; to cause a change in the character, thought or action of another'. We define conflict as 'the management of differences'." Negotiation, as defined by Lee E. Miller, author of *UP: Influence Power and the U Perspective—The Art of Getting What You Want*, is "the art of getting what we want in life and business."

Hornell says that "with these definitions in mind, conflict and negotiation can be viewed as more transactional around specific situations, whereas, influence is relational, a series of interactions over time requiring a deeper connection with others. Given this framework, we can say that influence is truly the art and practice of playing well with others with a higher purpose."

Hornell adds, "Leaders who play well with others know who they are and what they bring to the table. They have integrity because their internal values and beliefs are congruent with their external behavior–what you see is what you get. Influential leaders are not viewed as manipulative or only out for number one. They are strategic, with a keen sense of what is best for the organization, and what each party brings to the situation. In their dealings with others, effective influencers honor others by showing them respect and valuing them, while focusing on the best results for the business. They are able to be in the moment while keeping the end goal in mind.

"Preparation is a hallmark of influential leaders— clarifying what they want and why they want it, as well as considering what the other party wants and why they want it. If the influencers don't know what the other party wants, they must be willing to ask questions and listen for the story behind the response. The choice to listen and stay in learning mode builds trust and allows time for both parties to make necessary shifts and come to a mutually beneficially answer. Effective influencers understand that a solution forced upon another party is ineffective in the long run, and time spent preparing for the 'influence table' pays off."

For anyone who aspires to assume a leadership role in their organization, time spent learning how to more effectively influence others and to be a better negotiator, a related influencing skill, is time well spent. The greater your scope of responsibility the more you need the help of others to accomplish your objectives.

According to Lee E. Miller, your ability to gain the support of others is dependent on understanding how they see the world—what will motivate them to want to do what you want. This is what Miller refers to as the "U Perspective".

Most people simply assume that everyone sees the world the way he or she does. We think, if only we explain things better others will come around to our point of view. Even when we recognize that someone else may see a situation differently than we do, our first instinct usually is to try to persuade that person to see things our way. More often than not that approach does not work.

The U Perspective takes the opposite approach. Its effectiveness is not rooted in the ability to persuade others to change their views or adopt different values. Instead, its power comes from recognizing, and harnessing, what others already believe and want. The U Perspective allows you to get what you want by working within another person's belief system, rather than challenging it. To be able to influence someone, you need to discover what is important to that person. You need to learn to see things through his or her eyes. Once you understand how the person sees a situation you have the ability to construct, and present, options in a way that effectively influences what he or she does.

Showing how your proposal helps further the objectives of those people whose assistance you seek makes it easy to gain their support. People are motivated by many things. Money, friendship, a shared purpose, recognition, status, time, ease, helping others, fairness, teamwork, family, and challenge are among the values that you can appeal to when you seek to gain someone's help or support. What motivates each of us, though, is different depending on the situation and the other people involved.

How do you determine what will motivate someone? You listen. People will always tell you what is important to them, if you only listen. The more someone talks, the more information you will get, directly and indirectly about what is important to that individual. Once you understand someone's U Perspective, you can use that to gain his or her support. Not only will they help you, they will do so enthusiastically. What enables great leaders to inspire others is being able to identify shared values and appealing to those values in a way that gets people to want to help the leader achieve his or her stated goals. You cannot change someone's U Perspective anymore than you can swim against the tide for any length of time. But like riding a wave, if you harness the power of the U Perspective of those whose help you need, you can achieve great things.

SUMMARY:

Successful leaders....

1. Have a high degree of EQ in addition to their IQ.

2. Demonstrate by their actions the congruence of their values and beliefs– "what you see is what you get".

3. Are able to influence outcomes through and with others.

4. Engage people personally to establish professional relationships.

5. Understand and appreciate the U perspective.

6. Seek out diverse opinions and perspectives.

7. Don't take it personally.

CALL TO ACTION:

●Assess how approachable and how open to others' ideas and perspectives you are.

●Meet with a key individual in your organization to gain feedback on how you can manage if others do not embrace your ideas. Identify ways in which you can manage these situations to achieve mutual satisfaction.

●Actively solicit the perspective of a crucial associate for a current project/initiative so you have the broadest perspective to create the most successful outcome.

NOTES

NOTES

Rule #8:
Take Risks, Make Decisions

Rosina says that when she meets with male senior executives and she asks them what skills they would most like to see women in their organizations improve, they would almost always answer with: 1) I wish women would not take things so personally (as mentioned in Chapter 7), and 2) I wish they would be more confident in making decisions, or that they would make them faster. Rosina has heard these two things said so often they have borne out in the discussions held in WOMEN Unlimited programs. Many women are risk averse and fearful that the decision they make may be wrong. The idea of not being right one hundred percent of the time is hard for some women to accept. Also, many women prefer to make a decision that everyone will accept.

Great leaders are almost always great simplifiers who can cut through argument, debate, and doubt, to offer a solution everybody understands.

General Colin Powell

One of the exercises that WUI participants experience is: Imagine you are at lunch with a group of women and the wait staff hands each of you a menu. What typically is one of the first things women at this lunch will do when they look at the menu? They may peruse the menu quickly but we all know from experience that the first thing usually out of a woman's mouth is, "What are you going to have?" WUI participants usually have a lively discussion regarding the various reasons women ask this. We believe women ask this question because we possess a need for approval. Even the choice of what one eats seems to require approval. The reason we use this simple exercise is to drive a discussion around the fact that many women may be hesitant to make decisions without getting group approval in their workplaces. But all employees—men and women—need to make decisions with which not everyone will agree or support.

Making the time to think, reflect, and plan can make all of the difference in the decisions we make, and it can give us the confidence to act without fear. As you will read in this chapter, having a Plan B is highly recommended, and it has served each of us well. Jean says, "Knowing that if a decision I am making may not produce the results I've expected, I feel very comfortable knowing that I have done adverse consequences planning in order to easily implement Plan B."

Tammy Savoie, Senior Account Manager at Siemens PT & D, explains that at a WUI workshop she learned that "we should only bring up a problem or an issue if we can also provide a proposed solution. I had a big customer issue that my company was blaming on a third party that we had hired and the third party was blaming us. The customer didn't care who was at fault, they just wanted their system to work as promised." After months of finger pointing, Savoie took a risk and says she suggested Siemens pay for and perform a root cause analysis to determine what was causing the problem.

"As it turns out," Savoie says, "the customer's parameters had changed since we originally designed the system, and the customer was at fault." If she hadn't taken a risk, made a suggestion, and followed through with the decision, all three parties would still be suffering.

WHAT KIND OF RISK TAKER ARE YOU?

What kind of risk taker and decision maker are you? Are you willing to go out on the proverbial limb and suggest a "play" that your company could make to solve a problem? Some people, because of their styles or personalities, will make decisions whether they have the authority to do so or not. Others wait for permission. Which do you do most often? Are there areas where you could or should be making decisions but you are hesitant?

Ask yourself the following questions:

- How comfortable am I making decisions at work?
- How long does it usually take me to make a decision?
- How do I feel if the decision I make is wrong?
- How do I handle a decision that doesn't go as planned?

Many years ago the U.S. Army did a study to determine whether men or women make better decisions. The results showed that women make better decisions, ones that have a greater long-term impact, but it takes women too long to make their decisions. Women have a fear of decision-making and a fear of moving things forward. This comes mainly from their striving for perfection. Women's fears focus on making the right decision, as if there's only one correct answer. We never want to be wrong because we are afraid that will reveal to others that we aren't smart or worthy to be in our jobs. But for most problems, multiple resolutions exist. Don't waste so much time looking for THE right answer. In order to make a decision, get as much information as you can at the time, reach the best conclusion you can, and then change it later if you have to.

Jean says that one of her late husband's favorite sayings was, "The Puck is in the Net." While we weigh our options during the decision-making process, others around us are scoring. They are actively playing the game while we are hoping for a "time-out" so we can review all of the angles and collect data on previous similar decisions and their outcomes. Sometimes we just need to grasp the stick and shoot the puck as best we can toward the net. And if it bounces off the posts or the crossbar, so be it. It's an experience from which we can learn.

Failures often make our careers. When we learn from something not working well with Plan A and we can present Plan B or C or even D and fall back on the alternate plans, we will look like leaders who have thought through every scenario. Decisions need to be made as quickly as possible with the information available. Laure E. Park, Vice President, Communications and Investor Relations of Quest Diagnostics Incorporated, agrees. "I have increased the speed with which I make decisions," she says. "While I still include the appropriate analysis, I am speeding the process to avoid analysis paralysis. This has become increasingly important as my scope of responsibilities expand."

Because many decisions need to be made quickly, the decisions themselves need to be fluid, and so does the decision-making process. The art in decision-making allows us to pull on past experiences (experiential intuition) to project outcomes, and then to make adjustments as necessary. Yes, people may remember failures, but they will remember even more how the failure was handled and the risks that were taken to fix it. Being proactive in the recovery of faulty decisions can earn you positive marks and carry you far in your organization, perhaps even farther than always making the correct decision after examining the possible outcomes from every angle over long periods of time.

But women (way more than men) fear failure. Esteemed professor and gender communication specialist Deborah Tannen said that when men fail, they don't blame themselves. They blame external factors. When women fail, they first blame themselves. That fear of failure drives perfectionism and makes women spend too much time in decision-making. Fear drives perfectionism and perfectionism drives fear. Women need to get comfortable taking smart risks and then driving the decision forward to an effective outcome.

UNDERSTANDING RISK ASSESSMENT

Jack Yurish offers a simple method to effectively assess the probability and seriousness of things that could go wrong when it comes to decision-making. "Starting with a blank sheet I enumerate all the things that could go wrong. For each issue I complete an assessment as follows:

ISSUE (Probability x Seriousness = Impact)

P (1-10) x S (1-10) = I (10-100)

1= LOW, 10=HIGH

Using the scale of 1-10 assess the overall impact of each issue related to the various alternatives being considered. Once you have a feel for the overall impact of each alternative, you are in a much better position to decide to risk it or fix it. Very often the alternative that meets most of your objectives while presenting the least threatening adverse consequences becomes your best way to go."

Yurish says that an added benefit to doing risk assessment is that it gives you the opportunity for downside planning action (creating those Plan Bs, Cs, Ds, etc.) Kathleen Cashman, CEO and President of Cashman Consulting, LLC, says that one of the challenges for women that impact the quality of their decisions is not leaving enough evidence of thinking strategically. Yurish says his PxS=I process is "a useful tool for getting the adverse consequence naysayers on board, as it helps them better understand the irrationality of their blind resistance, especially when it comes to the probability of something happening or the seriousness if it does."

RISK PLANNING CHECKLIST

WOMEN Unlimited uses the following Risk Planning Checklist to help with the decision making process.

1. Goals
- What are the primary and secondary goals for taking this risk?
- How will making these decisions or goals affect you, your organization, and other key parties?
- How will you measure whether these goals have been achieved?

2. Problems
- What major barriers might you encounter?
- Who will resist, impede, or subvert your decision/risk the most?
- What, if anything, can you do to limit or prevent this?

3. Solutions
- Which problems can you avoid or prevent?
- How will you do this?
- Which problems can you limit, contain, or reduce? How will you do that?
- What can you do to survive problems you can't avoid, prevent, or limit?

4. Resources
- Which people are essential to implementing your plan?
- Which of their skills do you need?
- How can you enlist their wholehearted support?
- How much of their time do you need?
- What other resources (materials, equipment, money, etc.) do you need?

5. **Activities**
- What sequential steps will achieve your decision-making/risk-taking goals?
- How much time will each step require?
- What could sabotage your plans at each step?

THINKING STRATEGICALLY AS OPPOSED TO ONLY TACTICALLY

Yurish explains that the difference between strategy and tactics is that "stratagems refer to direction and position while tactics or tactical refers to the actions, methods, and/or practices employed to achieve that direction or positioning." In other words, you need one to have the other.

"The corporations, organizations, and individuals who possess the capability or skills of foresight, innovation, and risk-taking, in greater measures than others, seem to be more successful at spotting and/or creating opportunities for significant achievement, growth, contribution, and reward," explains Yurish. "They create the direction or theme which positions them for greater success. But strategy alone doesn't lead to success. Success requires equally innovative tactics, actions, and execution to support the strategy and to produce the anticipated results. There is a big distinction between setting the direction and making it happen. Both are required."

Look at some of our best-known American companies: Nike, Google, American Express, e-Bay, Colgate-Palmolive, DuPont, Microsoft, and others (including WUI). All of these companies understand what it takes to think and to position themselves strategically. Leaders who desire to become more effective in regard to determining strategies and tactics should study the aforementioned organizations and other well-run companies.

In his book, *Competing for the Future*, globally-renown consultant in strategic planning Gary Hamel, suggests people ask themselves questions to determine if they are strategically or tactically oriented. The questions include:

• Am I more of a maintenance engineer, keeping today's business humming along, or an architect imagining tomorrow's business?

• Do I promote more energy prolonging the past than I do to creating the future?

• How often do I lift my gaze out of the rut and consider what's out there on the horizon?

• What is the balance between hope and anxiety in my company (or my job)?

• What is the balance between confidence in our ability to find and [capitalize on] opportunities for growth and new business development?

Yurish says, "It is incumbent upon leaders, who wish to continue personal growth and effectiveness, to stay abreast of the evolving concepts of strategy and ways of implementing those strategies, so that their personal contributions to and rewards from the opportunity curve called 'life' will continue in a quantum manner."

TAKE SOME RISKS TO FURTHER YOUR CAREER

Michele Donato, Business Operations Manager at Microsoft, says that one of the biggest things she learned through WOMEN Unlimited was about taking risks and asking for what she wants. "I made a conscious effort to take more risks in my day to day work life because I knew taking more risks would help me grow. I realized the worst that could happen is that I could make a mistake. So I even added risks to my career development plan."

Donato was working in a secure business group when she was going through the LEAD program in 2007. In order to go grow her skills and to take some risks, she asked for a temporary assignment that would allow her to focus on skills she was looking to obtain. She met with the VP of her group and asked for guidance on roles that would help her grow based on identified areas. "At the end of six months, I had to make a decision on whether I wanted to grow in the new group," Donato says. "I asked myself what I had to lose and knew the worst thing that could happen was that I wouldn't like my new job. My advice to women is that if you are in your comfort zone, it is time to move on. You are no longer growing."

Donato believes that if you play it safe all of the time, and don't take risks with your decisions, your results will always remain safe. "For me, it's about the journey more than the end goal," she says.

Just because you made a mistake doesn't mean you are a mistake.

Georgette Mosbacher

For her, the biggest reward of taking risks and making decisions is how much she's learned. Dianna D. Wilusz, Managing Director, Private Equity Services at Craford Consulting, and a WUI Mentor, agrees. "My risk taking has become bolder in my own career. I have personally realized that opportunities are presented every day, so the most important thing is to show up and play fully."

A rather astute executive asked Donato during her executive interviews as a part of the LEAD Program, "Where do you see yourself when you retire? Once you figure that out, work backwards on what you want to accomplish in order to reach that goal." Working backwards involves a lot of risk and making many decisions. But in the end, as Donato says, "It will be worth it because you are driving towards your goal, both from a personal and a professional perspective. And if you slip up along the way, that's okay, too. Because you will always learn something as the result of your journey."

PITFALLS TO RISK TAKING AND DECISION MAKING

We believe that when people are feeling overwhelmed, tired, stressed, or are working at a 24-7 pace constantly, it is almost impossible for them to make rational, effective decisions. "In fact," Jean says, "it is not wise to make decisions without taking the time to focus on the decision that needs to be made. I encourage women in our programs to make sure they make the time each and every day to think. I recommend they put themselves on their calendars and to keep that appointment as if it were with one of their most important customers, clients, or senior executives." For only if we do this can we avoid the pitfall of making a rash decision.

Cashman says some other pitfalls in taking risks and decision-making include making assumptions (and then recording and tracking those), not networking to gain access to information at a strategic level, and not moving forward with information because you think you need to have all of it before you can make a decision. "Effective leadership includes the ability to make decisions on your own without permission all of the time," Cashman says. "Even if you made the wrong decision, you still took the chance to make that decision and that says something. Effective leadership skills demand that you be willing to take risks at all times."

Donato adds that taking the biggest risks and challenges and making those decisions can be frustrating since you may make mistakes or hit brick walls. You are in charge of your career through the risks you take and the decisions you make.

Because in the end, as lawyer and former president of Harvard University, A. Lawrence Lowell, said, "There is only one thing which will really train the human mind, and that is the voluntary use of the mind by the persons themselves. You may suggest to them, and above all, you may inspire them; but the only thing worth having is that which they get by their own exertion: and what they get is proportionate to the effort they put into it." Every decision we make and risk we take requires effort and the decisions that further our careers often require the most risk and effort.

SUMMARY:

Successful leaders...

1. Make the time to think about the decisions they need to make.

2. Demonstrate a high degree of confidence in the decisions they make.

3. Are able to gain support from critical allies for their decisions.

4. Understand that there are times everyone won't support the decision that must be made.

5. Understand that not all decisions will be 100% effective 100% of the time.

6. Use adverse consequence thinking to plan for potential problems.

7. Are very comfortable with Plan B thinking.

8. Are able to accept responsibility for decisions that did not meet expectations, learn from them, and move on.

OTTE · RACIOPPI · FERGUSON

CALL TO ACTION:

●Identify one area where you can strengthen your "risk-taking muscle".

●Identify someone who is very effective in managing risks and decision-making and meet with him/her over the next month to identify how you can learn another approach to strengthen your risk-taking skills.

●Meet with a critical ally for feedback on your risk-taking/decision-making abilities. Ask for specific feedback on if you demonstrate effective decision making/risk taking for your level in your organization. Identify one or two areas you can focus upon for your further development.

NOTES

NOTES

Rule #9:
Seed for the Future

In the Catalyst study referenced throughout this book, respondents said in hindsight they wished they had known more about how "to plan my goals and career in advance, learning about the next steps" and how "to find a good mentor/coach/sponsor." Doing these two things helps you seed for the future.

When Rosina first got involved with WOMEN Unlimited, it was in the role of corporate partner when she put two women with high potential into the program. And as these women went through the program, she watched them take charge of their careers and create a career plan. Rosina had always been frustrated by people who had abdicated their careers to others. She believed it was up to women to plot their courses in their organizations and in their lives.

> *Treat people as they are and they will remain that way. Treat them as though they already are what they can be, and you will help them become what they are capable of becoming.*
>
> Goethe

Women who took control of their careers by planning were more successful and more content. They found better ways around obstacles. This is one of the key things learned in WOMEN Unlimited: each employee must seed for her own future.

Also, as part of preparing for the future, you need to know what you bring to the organization and how that differentiates you from others. And then you need to make others aware of what skills and talents you possess and how those fit into what is valued by the company. When senior corporate leaders recognize your skills, then you'll be considered a viable candidate for a particular project or a particular role.   Another part of seeding for the future is ensuring others have been trained and have developed the skills needed to take your place. Rosina says, "You must be known as a developer of talent. If you're only in the game for yourself, then you'll be tethered to the job you are in. You must develop those around you."

Some people do this by mentoring, either on a formal or an informal basis. But mentoring isn't only about what you can contribute to someone else's life. The mentors in WOMEN Unlimited have said they have derived more value from those they've mentored than what they feel they've contributed. Mentoring gives a new and sometimes clearer perspective of what's going on in various parts of an organization. A senior manager who mentors can help re-establish his or her connection to what people think in the lower levels of the company. And even if you are mentoring people who work in other organizations, you can translate what is going on in their companies and in their careers into your own. Male mentors have developed an understanding of what it is like to be a female in certain work environments. One male mentor told Rosina that he knew his female employees were probably feeling the same way about things as the woman he was mentoring, but he realized they probably didn't feel comfortable talking to him because he was a man. He used this new understanding to make small changes that helped his female employees.

The last part of seeding for the future is to create an environment where the people around you can learn and grow. You can do this by being aware of obstacles and trying to diminish their impact for your team or other diverse groups. You can also do this by providing opportunities for employees to stretch their skills and talents, and to learn and develop new ones.

Donna Coulson, M.S., PCC, Northeast TEAM Manager at WOMEN Unlimited, says that to seed for your future, you need to focus on three distinct levels: you as a leader, your business unit, and your company. "To stay ahead of the curve in your field, use your internal and external peer network to track trends—and decipher what impact these trends will have on you, your industry, and your career. Go online and subscribe to one or two key industry publications. Build funding into your budget annually to attend a relevant conference or workshop. Better yet, bloom more widely and offer to be a speaker at a conference demonstrating your area of expertise to enhance your visibility. For trends, visit www.worldfuturesociety.com," says Coulson.

Michelle Chiantera, Manager of U.S./Canada Channel Marketing at Cisco, believes that in order to focus on yourself, you need to know your expertise—what you are great at—and build this into your professional brand (and this will also help you seed for the future). "When you know if you are a great speaker, writer, networker, etc. in your organization, you will get pulled into projects that need your expertise. WOMEN Unlimited helped me figure out what this meant. From there you need to document your career plan. If you don't write it down you will have nothing to go back to." Chiantera created a career wheel in PowerPoint, and she reviews it every year and makes changes as necessary. "It should not be a static document, but it should help you see where you need to get more experience. My career wheel displays who I am and what I'm faithfully offering Cisco."

Chiantera's career wheel starts with a statement of what position she aspires to and in what time frame to which she hopes to achieve that position. The next slide shows personal considera-tions/motivations, followed by a slide of functional focus options, then job location preferences, then general job characteristics, then specific information about Cisco's structure, and finally ways she either has or could expand her general marketing skill set. Figure 9-1 is an example of that last slide.

DEVELOP THOSE WHO PLAY ON YOUR TEAM

Part of focusing on you as a leader is to always develop those on your team. Patty Watson, Senior Technology Executive, SVP at Bank of America, said that being in the LEAD Program was a turning point for her. "When I was in the LEAD Program, I had thirty people working for me. Now I have almost eight hundred. I can relate to Rosina's frustration because I was one of those people who was-n't actively taking charge of my career. But through WOMEN Unlimited I realized the importance of having a succession plan in place. If you don't, it limits your mobility." Watson said she wanted to be set apart from everyone else and be better than everyone else. But she found that if your company cannot see anyone else but you in your job, then you will get stuck there.

"I always make sure I know exactly what I'm doing and that I give my folks opportunities," she says. "My peers call it 'Patty Watson's School of Talent Sharing', meaning I always have a plan on how to backfill people. I hold people very accountable, and when my people move on, they do very well for themselves, and they do great things for our company. Success for me is watching the people I'm responsible for attain their career objectives."

Coulson seconds this by explaining, "To seed for the future, you must have talent consistently in your pipeline. Development is ongoing and never ends—just like cultivating a garden season after season. Grow a successor in your garden to replace yourself as leader, so you can move on to broaden yourself or to move up the organization. The flower may or may not reside in your garden. When I worked as a Training Manager at Prudential, I was astounded when my top two trainers opted not to move into management. They liked training, not managing others. Through my network, I identified a colleague in another location who wanted to broaden his background and eagerly assumed this role.

All too often we are giving people cut flowers when we should be teaching them to grow their own plants.

John Gardner

"Also, when developing your people, hold them accountable for sharing their key learnings with colleagues when they return from conferences or workshops."

MENTORS AND MENTORING ARE ESSENTIAL IN SEEDING FOR THE FUTURE

In addition to encouraging your team members, part of seeding for the future is making sure you and your employees have mentors. "I encourage high potentials to identify a mentor within the broader organization, not necessarily within their function of the business," Chiantera says. "This not only helps expand your network but gives a very different perspective on our or your exposure to the business."

Laura Browne, TEAM Program Manager in the Western Region, says, "You can't wait for your boss to develop you. It's up to you to decide what you want to do with your career and plan your next moves. Then talk to your boss to get feedback and support. Your boss can't read your mind. Managers today are typically so busy that they don't have time to focus on your next steps unless you take the initiative and clearly state what you want to do." You have to be proactive in your career.

Watson has created a career development presentation and part of it explains to people how to network and how to get a mentor. She created this presentation so people could avoid the mistakes she made early in her career. "When I have people make development plans, I have them identify five people they don't know. Then I try to stretch their

187

OTTE · RACIOPPI · FERGUSON

associations by giving them new opportunities based on what I think their potentials are. I give them tasks they haven't done before but where they can use their skill sets. This usually works but sometimes people end up in roles for which they aren't suited." Watson said this then becomes a learning experience for them and for her.

"I remember telling my manager after a WOMEN Unlimited session," says Watson, "that he was really going to regret sending me there because I was turning into a monster. I sent out my career expectations to him and within one month I got everything I had asked for. And I never would have had the courage to ask if it wasn't for the LEAD Program." Since then, Watson has encouraged all of the people she mentors to do the same.

Nicola Foster, HR Manager at a European Market Leading Financial Services Company, developed a career outcome to find a mentor "who already had a good record for developing other people; had a wide range of current skills and knowledge to pass on; had a genuine interest in seeing women advance", and who possessed a number of other qualities. She uniquely handled finding a mentor by starting her search on the Internet, where she came across Jean's book *Changing the Corporate Landscape: A woman's guide to cultivating leadership excellence.*

Upon reading the book, Foster thought she had found the mentor she was seeking, so she summoned her courage and sent Jean an e-mail. At WUI, we tell people that oftentimes they have not because they ask not. Jean, after a phone call, agreed to mentor her. Three years later, Foster says that the advice she's received, including "let go of the outcome," "just because you can doesn't mean you should," "continue to build that CV and have it at the ready as you never know when opportunity presents itself," has helped her career flourish, and she's now paying it forward by being a mentor to others.

UNDERSTAND EXTERNAL AND INTERNAL FORCES

The final part of seeding for your future is to understand how external forces and internal personnel affect your business climate. Coulson remarks, "Gardens vary year to year depending on cultivation, temperatures, weather patterns, and soil. Business, too, varies year to year in international, national, local economies, politics, or customer preferences and behaviors. Grandma was right when she declared, 'Nothing ever stays the same.' So, plan for deviations—successes, downtrends or moderate growth. Be flexible and resilient like a rose—roses look delicate on the outside but those thorns protect it from the environment and predators."

Coulson adds, "During times of change, engage your people in experiences that stretch them and encourage them to be change-able and resilient—the garden that weathers the storm. When Keyspan Energy was going through a merger with National Grid, instead of postponing development of their people until after the merger, we agreed to put them in TEAM as the merger was executed. Four of their six participants volunteered for Change Management Committees to lead this transition. They helped define the change and the new organi-zation—a better perspective than waiting and won-dering, 'What will happen to me?' As Mahatma Gandhi once said, 'Be the change you want to see in the world'."

Any type of seeding for the future and creating change involves taking risks. Watson's original career was in the Air Force, where she said she learned that leaders take responsibility, they take care of their people, and they remove roadblocks. Chiantera says she seeds for the future by doing three things with her team: she tries to empower them, she establishes trust, and she sincerely cares about their careers. "I have a commitment to help people who are committed and motivated," she states. "Louanne Tierney taught me that it is okay to make mistakes as long as those mistakes become opportunities. People can be uncomfortable about asking for help so they may avoid taking risks. This can be a career pitfall."

So Chiantera, like Watson, assigns her people to short and long term projects that will provide them with growth opportunities. "Sometimes I assign people to special projects with the CIO or their peers or other senior managers so they'll get exposure and others will know who they are," Watson says. She learned this from experience. "The CIO in the company's development program said he hadn't seen my name [when I received my executive level promotion]. So he wanted me to network with five specific people. This helped my career." And now she's paying this advice forward and seeding for her future and that of others.

SUMMARY:

Successful Leaders...

1. Regularly reassess their contributions and skills to prepare them for career opportunities and growth.

2. Have a succession planning process in place to recruit and foster the development of high potential employees/associates.

3. Create for others an environment in which to succeed and assume responsibilities.

4. Communicate their ideas for both their career growth and that of their associates with their critical alliances.

5. Mentor and coach others to assist them with their goals.

6. NETWORK...NETWORK...NETWORK!

CALL TO ACTION:

●Set aside periodic development "think time" by blocking off time on your calendar when you will not be distracted. Reflect on your career goals, review your development plan, assess your development over the past few months and make adjustments as needed.

●Identify two key individuals who can provide insight, feedback, and support for your development. Schedule a meeting with them over the next month.

●Set a plan to develop others by identifying one individual to mentor. Establish a framework to work with this individual. Set timelines to ask for feedback on how this has helped the person.

●Identify networking opportunities to attend and meet three new people.

Figure 9-1

Personal Considerations/Motivations

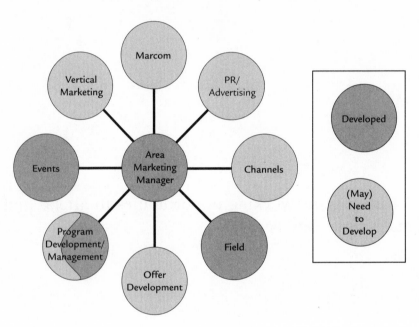

NOTES

NOTES

Rule #10:
Enjoy the Game

After having had the opportunity to observe thousands of women who have participated in the WUI programs nationwide over the past fifteen years Rosina and Jean share concerns that despite the dedication and hard work of many women, they are simply not enjoying the game they have chosen to play. Many are so busy practicing and playing that they do not make time to step back and enjoy the fruits of their labor. They do not notice or examine how their contribution to the game has been changing the corporate landscape.

With the increasing advent of an expanding global workplace and technological advancements, the 24-7 workday has become the norm, and many women are choosing this mode of operation. They play the game as if every move they make is critical, and they must be involved in every play, which in turn makes them become exhausted employees.

> *To love what you do and feel that it matters, how could anything be more fun?*
>
> Katharine Graham

Women have shared that even when they do take a vacation (and there are those who never do use the vacation time they have earned) they still feel compelled to stay connected and involved.

The United Nations' International Labor Organization study showed that on average Americans work approximately two thousand hours per year. (In some industries—such as law and high tech—the standard is even higher than that.) If you are going to spend so much time in the office or in front of your computer or doing things related to your job, shouldn't you, at a very minimum, enjoy what you are doing?

Who says you can't have fun at work or enjoy your job? Yet so many people think of their occupations as work—dull, must-get-through-them tasks—or as a swamp that is slowly sucking away their joy.

WUI asks women who are not enjoying what they are doing, how long before you will not be fit to play? What kind of role model are you for others? Do you have a daughter, niece, or other young woman in your life who looks up to you and says, "I want to be just like her"? Or, do the people in your life see you as a stressed out person who doesn't enjoy her existence?

Jean shared in her first book, *Changing the Corporate Landscape: A woman's guide to cultivating leadership excellence*, that in order for plants to continue to bloom, grow, and create a wonderful landscape, they must have dormant times to absorb nutrients. As women in the workplace, it is vital to be dormant at times, to reflect, renew, and recharge, to ensure continued growth so we can contribute our best efforts.

THE POWER OF SELF-ACCEPTANCE

But often during our dormant times we become critical of ourselves. How frequently do you say to yourself, "I look fat," or do you ask yourself, "Why am I always saying such stupid things?" or "I wonder what he thinks of me?" When we say these things to ourselves, we are giving over our power to external sources. Tieraona Low Dog, M.D., Director of Fellowship and Clinical Assistant Professor at Arizona Center for Integrative Medicine, says, "You may be caught in a self-defeating pattern that limits your ability to experience real joy and true wellbeing.

"There is no question that we are living in stressful times," Dr. Low Dog points out. "Given the growing uncertainty in our world, women are concerned with their health, financial security, and the wellbeing of loved ones. Many believe they can reduce the uncertainty, and thus the stress, by working harder, earning more money, losing more weight, taking more vitamins, being more, having more, more, more. But how many people have you known that 'had it all'—money, fame, success, love—and wound up on anti-depressants or tranquilizers, in unhappy relationships, gotten divorced, or gone through years of therapy? On the other hand, we have all heard stories of people who survived horrific conditions in concentration or in refugee camps, endured years of physical abuse and other traumas and have managed to retain their joy and hopes."

Gina Flaig (back in Chapter 6) commented on how she was a workaholic, had completely lost touch with her priorities, and had discontinued most of her personal relationships. She realized how stressful things were at work, and that she was the only one who could take control of her life.

American humorist James Thurber encourages us to "not look back in anger or forward in fear, but around in awareness." Dr. Low Dog says that the direction we lean in times of stress, our tipping point, lies deep within. For we choose our response, and that decision is based to a large degree upon how we approach our relationship with self, or our degree of self-acceptance. Self-acceptance is having a positive self-regard or a general sense of happiness in oneself."

What Flaig discovered is that if we show up unengaged, overworked, and overstressed, we will start to repel people. They won't want to be around us, and as Rosina says, "This could be the biggest detriment to our careers as leaders."

We need to create an environment where people are comfortable with us and where they feel free to dialogue with us. A crucial part of creating that environment involves accepting yourself. You have to do that before you can attract others to you. Dr. Low Dog says, self-acceptance "is loving who you are now. It's a pact you make with yourself to appreciate, accept, and support who you are in this moment—including those parts of yourself that you would eventually like to change... People who are unhappy take defeat and magnify it." This can be a repelling factor.

"Don't create hesitancy in people to reveal things to you," Rosina advises, "especially things that are critical. Be open to hearing valued input, from everyone, regardless of their functional area or the level they are in." We've all been in companies where something has happened and people around us say, "I could have told you that would happen." And the something that happened usually happens because a key employee didn't know x or y. "A critical leadership role is to invite dialogue before the 'something' happens."

In order to know and accept yourself—and to draw others to you—Dr. Low Dog offers the following three suggestions. First, accentuate your strengths. Write down those words that describe you—confident, impulsive, caring, aggressive, creative, etc.—

and keep adding to your list over time. Reflect on what motivates you to think and act the way you do. Chip away at your excuses and defenses.

Second, nourish inspiration. Write down those characters or people that speak to your dreams and desires. Read books, find mentors, and look for those who nourish your talents. The archetypes you embrace and the daydreams that recur can reveal what is impor- tant to you, what you want to accomplish, and who you are.

> *Act as if what you do makes a difference. It does.*
>
> William James

Third, be a truth-teller. To tell the truth, you must be willing to take down your defenses, and say the things that are hard to say, do the things that are hard to do, and see the things that are hard to see. Let the truth of who you are and what you are guide your actions.

As Chinese philosopher Lao Tzu said, "Knowing others is wisdom, knowing yourself is enlighten- ment."

ENJOY YOUR WORK AND HELP OTHERS ENJOY THEIRS

At WUI, we challenge the women in our programs by asking them tough questions, including if they are enjoying their work. And sometimes, during these programs, women are encouraged to find better roles for themselves within their organizations. And these new roles better utilize their skills and make the women feel like their jobs are now something they can enjoy and feel much better doing.

Browne says that work is not a dress rehearsal. It is a part of life and if you are not happy with what you are doing at work, it is up to you to change it. No one is going to do that for us. "When I started getting stressed at work it was a great opportunity for me to step back and analyze what I was doing and what I should have been doing. This usually means I've been focusing on the wrong things, not on my strengths or things I'm truly interested in. When I am happy, my customers and my company benefit. By re-aligning yourself with your work and asking yourself what you enjoy most about your job, you can get back on track."

When Flaig realized how much she was no longer enjoying the landscape, she made changes and started to cultivate a personal garden: redeveloping friendships, finding a love interest and getting married, and eventually having kids. And she thanks WUI for helping her readjust her priorities.

FEED YOUR SOUL WITH SUCCESS

Rosina remarks, "We need to feed our souls with our successes." Do you remember when you were a child and your mother put your A+ paper or your artwork on the refrigerator? Part of having fun in the office is celebrating our successes. Verbally putting the success out there for everyone to see and admire, and also "posting" the successes of others. Starting meetings with the positives makes such an impact, as does spending equal time on the good things and the challenges.

Part of a leader's job is creating the fun in the organization. And this includes talking about what worked well. (You might even call it "Noteworthy News", as Rosina does.) In our rushed lives we often skip this part, focusing only on the problems, but doing that day after day and week after week drains the joy from the organization.

Bonnie McAreavy, Vice President and Chief Risk Officer at Prudential, has had the words "This Is Fun" in bold, foot-high, red letters framed and hanging in her various offices for years. "It's a good reminder for me, and for others, and while I can't say all my positions through the years have been laugh out loud fun, I can say I've enjoyed every one of them, and tried to find ways to help others enjoy their works and lives, too." Even comedians state they take their work seriously, but not themselves, so much.

It doesn't take much to have fun at work, McAreavy says, "Just a sense of humor, an occasional bit of whimsy, a genuine interest in the people we work with; this goes such a long way toward helping everyone take the daily challenges in stride."

Jean adds that WUI has a guide they give to all employees and associates that outlines the organization's core values. Part of this includes "Be committed to creating an experience for all of those with whom we interact that meets or exceeds their expectations... Be dedicated to creating an environment that seeks to help others find solutions, exercise initiative, and make decisions; and be an example of enjoying and celebrating roles and achievements."

One example of someone who has done this is a woman who went through the very first WUI program in New York. Jean explains that the woman was intelligent—she had earned two Ph.D.s and was now a very intense chemist at a global consumer products company. But she was clearly unhappy. She was a workaholic with no social life when she came to WUI, and she claimed to be overworked and constantly focused on her tasks.

Jean says, "At the end of the year, she was selected by her group as the person most changed by the WUI experience. She had created a more conducive environment and had carved out a personal life. She was more productive and more fulfilled." At graduation, the woman stood in front of the group and explained all of the changes she had experienced during the year. At the end of her speech she said, "The most important thing I learned, I learned from Jean Otte, and that is this: It's only toothpaste."

Jean repeats this story at all of the WUI programs. Because the most important thing for most of us to realize at each day's end is that very little of what we do in the office is so intense that it results in life or death. It's only toothpaste.

Rosina shares how she learned this lesson during a very difficult time. "This was my first management role and we were in the midst of a large workforce reduction. I was in the process of finalizing the details for the closing of one of our largest plants, reviewing the details of the separation plans, when my boss walked into my office and asked, 'Are you having fun?' I must have given him the funniest look because he started laughing and said, 'I know we are going through a difficult time, but you need to ask yourself, 'Why did I come here today?' He helped me realize that I was wearing my concern and misery like a shield, and in my role, that was dangerous. My staff, as well as the organization, needed me to present a positive voice that reassured those remaining in the company."

SUMMARY:

Successful leaders...

1. Understand the need to reflect and renew to ensure their continued growth and development.

2. Are role models for how they are making a difference.

3. Demonstrate their passion and enjoyment for what they do.

4. Inspire others to enjoy what they are doing.

5. Make the time to praise their employees/associates for their contributions.

6. Encourage their associates to take time to celebrate their achievements.

CALL TO ACTION:

●Assess your corporate reputation—not only on the work you complete but more importantly how others feel working with you. Identify two key individuals to provide you with their insight.

●Evaluate your current role. Consider your effectiveness. How are you playing to your strengths and how are you demonstrating your passion? Check in with others to validate your perception and/or to identify gaps.

●Establish a periodic meeting (formal or informal) to celebrate successes and to acknowledge others.

OTTE · RACIOPPI · FERGUSON

NOTES

NOTES

NOTES

Meet
The
Authors

Jean M. Otte

Jean Otte is founder and Chief Executive Officer of WOMEN Unlimited, Inc. and author of *Changing the Corporate Landscape: A Woman's Guide to Cultivating Leadership Excellence.* WOMEN Unlimited, Inc. is a nationally recognized resource for cultivating leadership excellence. Fortune 1000 companies partner with WOMEN Unlimited, Inc. to identify and develop success strategies for high potential female leaders.

Prior to founding WOMEN Unlimited, Inc. in 1994, Jean was an officer and Corporate Vice President for National Car Rental System, Inc. During her 30 years in the corporate world, Jean held management positions with McDonald's, Gillette and The Bell System before joining National Car Rental in 1980.

As a past President of the Society of Consumer Affairs Professionals (SOCAP), she led an international organization designed to foster and maintain the integrity of business in consumer dealings. Jean was selected and received certification as an examiner for the Malcolm Baldrige National Quality Award in 1992.

Jean is frequently requested to give keynote presentations and conduct workshops for organizations and governmental agencies worldwide. She has been featured in *Barron's, Business Week, Bloomberg News,* CBS, CNN, CNBC, NBC, *The Chicago Tribune, Fortune, Fast Co. Magazine, The New York Post, The New York Times, The Wall Street Journal Report,* and *Working Woman* and *CIO* magazines, among others. She has been honored by Lifetime Television, the Committee for 200, the Y.W.C.A. and Girls Inc. in recognition for her efforts in helping women to cultivate leadership excellence.

A native of Great Britain, Jean immigrated to the U.S. after graduating from St. Julians College in Newport, Wales with a degree in elementary education.

Rosina L. Racioppi
President and COO
WOMEN Unlimited, Inc.

Rosina Racioppi is President and Chief Operating Officer for WOMEN Unlimited, Inc., a nationally recognized resource for cultivating leadership excellence. Fortune 1000 companies partner with WOMEN Unlimited, Inc. to identify and develop success strategies for high potential female leaders. In her role, Rosina is responsible for ongoing business development and overall management of programs nationwide for WOMEN Unlimited. WOMEN Unlimited has been featured in *Business Week, Bloomberg News*, CNN, CNBC, *Chicago Tribune, Wall Street Journal Report* and *Fast Company*, *Working Women* and *CIO* magazines. Lifetime Television and the Committee for 200 and the Y.W.C.A. have honored WOMEN Unlimited's leadership development programs in recognition of its efforts on achieving parity in the workplace.

Prior to joining WOMEN Unlimited, Rosina held executive management positions in human resources and has extensive experience in Organization Planning and Development, Compensation and Benefits, Training and Development, Safety, Quality Management, Staffing and Employee Relations. Rosina has held positions with Degussa Corporation, Nextran (a division of Baxter Corporation), Technical Wire Products, and Beechwood Data Systems, Inc.

Rosina has served on the advisory panel for the American Management Association. In addition, Rosina is an active member of the SHRM (Society of Human Resource Managers), The American Society of Training and Development and The New Jersey Human Resources Planning Group.

Rosina is a graduate of Michigan State University with a Bachelors Degree in Criminal Justice. Rosina is certified in the Hay Job Evaluation Process and the Crosby Total Management System.